D0946438

# Continuing Education in Action

RESIDENTIAL CENTERS FOR LIFELONG LEARNING

Residential Centers for Continuing Education, such as the pictured "Kellogg Center" at Michigan State University, are making social, cultural, and economic impressions upon the American scene.

# Continuing Education in Action

## RESIDENTIAL CENTERS FOR LIFELONG LEARNING

HAROLD J. ALFORD, PH.D.,
Director, Departments of Independent Study,
Off-Campus Classes, and Special Courses,
University of Minnesota
for the
W. K. KELLOGG FOUNDATION
Battle Creek, Michigan

JOHN WILEY & SONS, INC.
New York · London · Sydney · Toronto

Copyright © 1968 by John Wiley & Sons, Inc.

All rights reserved. No part of this book may be reproduced by any means, nor transmitted, nor translated into a machine language without the written permission of the publisher.

Library of Congress Catalog Card Number: 68-31643
SBN 471 02220 9
Printed in the United States of America

# Preface

Through the years of its existence the W. K. Kellogg Foundation has promoted the application of knowledge as the chief means of narrowing the gap between the creation of information and its use for the public good. No program or movement that we have assisted has been more consistent with our application of knowledge philosophy than Continuing Education.

We have watched with pleasure the growth and evolution of ten Kellogg-aided residential centers designed to expedite university-oriented education for adults. Such prototype Centers for Continuing Education have made social, cultural, and economic impressions on the American scene—and the idea has taken root in that approximately eighty similar centers have been established independently by universities over the nation, with the promise of many more in the future.

Such mushrooming reflects a modern era in which change is more characteristic than continuity. Almost as many people have been born since 1950 as inhabited the whole planet in 1900. More than half the jobs and occupational areas open to a young man starting his career today did not exist when his father was a young man. It is estimated that a worker now entering the labor force at age 20 will go through seven major retraining periods in a forty-year career. The "half-life" of a physicist is now ten years, which means that half of what he knows today will be obsolete ten years from now and half of what he will need to know ten years ahead has not yet been discovered. At the far end of life's gamut, longevity has made a gift of added years to millions of men and women.

In response to such relatively new phenomena, the Foundation has expended more than $20 million in helping to expand the Continuing Education movement. Since the grants in the early 1950s to help establish the Kellogg Center for Continuing Education at Michigan State University, several score of proposals for similar aid have been received from tax-supported as well as private universities. In carefully considering all such proposals, we have, as a condition of our assistance, insisted on Continuing Education programs being in the context of universities with great intellectual resources and services—and not, as in some requests sent to us, under the umbrella of institutions with few resources. The influence of such Centers may vary from statewide to regional to national and even international scope. "The well is deep" in university-oriented education for adults, and, lest more harm than good be done, there must be a capacious reservoir of creative assets at every Center.

At a meeting at the Chicago Center attended by Directors of Kellogg-assisted Centers, in addition to several leaders of the field and representatives of the Foundation, we made the point: "The Foundation lacks the money to replicate Continuing Education Centers over the country, but we have an obligation to help establish guidelines that will aid people and institutions desiring to replicate the Centers."

Accordingly, the book to which these lines are a preface is intended to be helpful to universities that contemplate establishment of Centers for Continuing Education. It should appeal to educators at various levels who will be interested in a new and vibrant kind of education. In lesser but still important degree the book is pointed at an audience consisting of industrial corporations that are finding employee training and retraining programs a "must." Citizens with intellectual curiosity will read with appreciation the delineation of a movement vital to American progress in a new, almost bewildering, age.

In a how-it-was-done, how-to-do-it vein, the author, Dr. Harold Alford of the University of Minnesota, has sketched the origins of adult education and then has focused on the requisite planning for Continuing Education facilities and programming. He has outlined the myriad activities of a dedicated group of Center Directors, indicating their successes and their mistakes, and he has not neglected to describe in empathic detail the men and women participants who are the real reason-to-be of Continuing Education. Literally hundreds of thousands of adults today have gone back to school for brief periods to learn about scientific, economic, and social advances that can help them lead more useful and satisfying lives. It is to these people—and to the many more who will attend Continuing Education sessions in the future—that this book is dedicated.

EMORY W. MORRIS, Chairman of the Board
W. K. Kellogg Foundation

*Battle Creek, Michigan*
*September, 1968*

# Contents

# Continuing Education in Action

## RESIDENTIAL CENTERS FOR LIFELONG LEARNING

# Introduction

This year thirty million adults—one-fourth of the population of the United States over twenty-one—go back to school. Numerous institutions and agencies, private and corporate, are helping to make possible this massive expression of man's desire to learn. In just one segment of the movement private industry alone spends at least eighteen billion dollars annually for employee training and retraining programs, more than half the total public school budget and six times the amount appropriated by all the states for higher education in 1967–1968. Education can no longer be considered solely as a cure for ignorance through a prescription calling for a number of years in formal schoolwork. As John W. Gardner, former Secretary of Health, Education and Welfare, has said: "We have abandoned the idea that education is something that takes place in a block of time between six and eighteen (or twenty-two) years of age. It is lifelong." Technological change demands re-education in order to keep up. Technological change creates leisure time demanding to be filled. Adult education is the fastest growing sector of American education.

Yet adults are not just tall children who can be reprocessed through the same old youth-educating machine. Gardner adds: "We have abandoned the idea that education is something that can occur only in a classroom." Even "adult education" seems to imply a point of division between education in childhood and education in maturity. A new term is needed to suggest the single integrated process from prekindergarten to postretirement demanded by the knowledge explosion of the twentieth century. A more appropriate term is Continuing Education.

## FOCUS ON UNIVERSITY CENTERS

This book does not attempt to explore the whole merging world of continuing education which has potential horizons encompassing all knowledge

1

and all mankind. Its focus is on a single institutional form, *the university Continuing Education center,* and particularly on ten such pioneering institutions that came into being through the financial assistance of the W. K. Kellogg Foundation. Continuing Education in this setting has been defined as "continuing study by adults, utilizing periodic learning experiences within a university environment, and featuring a specially designed facility."

The first of the Kellogg-assisted centers was built at Michigan State University in 1951. The Georgia, Nebraska, and Oklahoma Centers followed, each located on the campus of a state university. Two private universities, Chicago and Notre Dame, were then given Kellogg Foundation assistance in establishing centers for Continuing Education on their campuses, and England's Oxford University, another of the great seats of classical learning, was also assisted in developing its "centre" for Continuing Education. Three additional centers are still in planning or construction stages, one a New England Center located on the campus of the University of New Hampshire but representing a consortium effort of the public universities of the six New England states, another an International Center for Continuing Education at Columbia University, and the most recent, "Kellogg West" at California State Polytechnic College, Kellogg-Voorhis Campus, at Pomona.

These ten centers for Continuing Education, financially assisted by the Kellogg Foundation, were conceived of as *residential* Continuing Education facilities; that is, they are virtually self-contained adult colleges with auditoriums and seminar rooms created especially to serve adult clientele and with comfortably appointed, tastefully decorated modern sleeping rooms and dining facilities. In addition, each of these centers is part of a great university whose total academic resources constitute the study environment made available to the adult continuing learner. Thus, from Michigan State to Oxford the conference content in centers for Continuing Education can encompass the range of human concerns in the complex milieu of mid-Twentieth Century global society.

## THE ONLY THING PERMANENT IS CHANGE

Less than two hundred years ago most Americans were farmers; today, only a small percent of the population is engaged in the production of food on the farm. Yet in states such as Nebraska and Oklahoma, oriented in past decades to agriculture, the majority of the adult education budget and efforts of the state universities were still directed toward agriculture in 1950 despite the impact of considerable industrialization in recent years. Certain pioneer practices had persisted, but so had the educational ways of a former era:

the one-room school, the inadequately trained teacher, the pitifully small store of out-of-date books and educational literature.

In Georgia and the Southeast a different set of circumstances—the heritage of a single crop economy and plantation society—had hampered educational advances; illiteracy was widespread, poverty was visible across the dusty red fields and in the crumbling hill and town cottages; and social unrest was a vast malignant growth, arrested but not dormant.

No longer held in place by a stable economy and clearly delineated occupational and social roles, the people of the South and Midwest began to move in the late thirties and the forties: from the farms to the towns, from the towns to the cities, and from the cities of their own areas to the industrial complexes of the East Coast and the Great Lakes. Adding to the impact and tension of change were government projects: the Tennessee Valley Authority and the Missouri Basin development programs. Titanic electric power complexes, flood control projects, and forest, wildlife and recreational programs, were aimed at promoting improved agricultural practices and clearing the way for balanced industrial development. Spawned by the intense activity of World War II, atomic and space age projects began to spread sprawling factories across the land where cotton, wheat and corn were once the staples. Highly sophisticated, these industries brought with them the demand for new educational and technical training resources. Thus, at midcentury, the face of the land was characterized by the restless surge of people into new environments for which they were not prepared socially, economically, and educationally.

The educational imperative was clear. Joseph K. Hart had put it well when he said:

"We may as well admit that it is not the education of children that can save the world from destruction; it is the adult who must be released from his provincial mindedness, his animistic prejudices, his narrow customs, his obsolete habits; it is the adult who must be given the chance to become free in a world of science, tolerance, human sympathy, and intelligent organization."

It was in response to this imperative that the first Kellogg Center was opened on the Michigan State University campus in 1951, to be followed during the next seventeen years by nine other Kellogg-assisted centers dedicated to the Continuing Education of adults. During those years, the presence and the programs of these dramatic facilities have had a profound influence on the direction of university Continuing Education throughout the United States. Many other campus-based, as well as industry-, profession-, and church-sponsored residential continuing education centers, have come into existence during the period, with most of them, to some degree at least, indebted to the Kellogg-assisted centers for their inspiration, design, and/or program.

This book, however, is not an attempt to record and compare all of the activities and methods of several-score centers, nor even of the ten Kellogg-assisted university centers for Continuing Education; neither is it a complete appraisal of their merits and demerits. What follows is simply the story of the ten centers; what they are, how they came to be, what they do, some of their strengths and weaknesses, and where they may be going. The material has been gathered through a search of records, personal observation, and interviews. Even in fictionalized passages, where some license has been exercised in the changing of names and the designation of dialogue, the presentation is as accurate in spirit and detail as the author could make it.

Continuing Education is a great new frontier of human activity. Here is the story of how one aspect of it began and developed.

CHAPTER 1

# Adult Learning in an Adult Environment: the Role of the Continuing Education Center

On a bright summer day a sleek jet aircraft from Washington, D.C., entered the landing pattern above Chicago's O'Hare field and nosed warily through the viscous haze that obscured the broad runways below. Two smartly dressed, attaché-case bearing passengers entered a waiting limousine. The driver tucked the dust cloth he had been using into the glove compartment and joined the six lanes of cars smoking along the freeway. Later he swung over to the lakeshore drive and eventually came to a gracefully columned modern building on the edge of an aging district, separated from the neo-Gothic quadrangles at the University of Chicago by a grassy midway, reminder of the turn-of-the-century world's fair.

Dust swirled from the gutter and scraps of paper tumbled along the sidewalk as the two hurried up the broad steps, across the spacious promenade, through the glass doors, and into the attractive red-carpeted lobby. A red-jacketed bellman took their bags and escorted them to the elevator and their second-floor twin bedroom, arranged so that the beds served as sofas when made up. One of the men brushed a spot of soot from his white cuff as the other adjusted the air conditioner to a comfortable temperature. They spread some of the papers from their attaché cases on the desk and bed. The heading on the printed program which one picked up for closer scrutiny was:

**NATIONAL CONFERENCE
ON AIR POLLUTION PREVENTION
UNIVERSITY OF CHICAGO CENTER FOR CONTINUING EDUCATION**

One smiled—a little grimly. "Our laboratory's outside," he said.
The other nodded. "Well, they've brought thirty of us 'experts' together

5

for the next ten days, and these are mighty fine working quarters. If we're ever going to talk our way toward a solution, now's the time."

Later that fall at the Nebraska Center for Continuing Education on the College of Agriculture campus of the University of Nebraska in Lincoln, eighteen dentists sat in the comfortably upholstered chairs of a small conference room and listened attentively while a distinguished colleague lectured and demonstrated with portable equipment and colored slides some of the latest developments in roentgenology. In another wing of the same building, the Hall of Youth, two hundred and five young people were attending a two-day rural youth institute during which they heard farm leaders and experts discuss the prospects for young people in agriculture and agri-business.

South from Lincoln, across the Kansas wheat fields, a cluster of buildings on the campus of the University of Oklahoma was the scene of a National Science Foundation-sponsored institute on esoteric concepts of petroleum product utilization in space-age technology. The small group of scientists was living, eating, sleeping, and working in the Hall of Advanced Studies, one building of the complex known as the Oklahoma Center for Continuing Education. Additional components of the four-million-dollar, twenty-acre "adult campus" included the "Forum," a three-winged structure of hexagonal conference rooms, ranging from those with a capacity of twenty-five to the largest seating six hundred persons; a seventy-two, twin-bedroom "Sooner House," providing living accommodations; the six-hundred capacity "Commons" dining hall, with its four mezzanine banquet rooms; ten duplex cottages spaced along one side of the site to house families; and a two-story administration building, the locale for planning and supervision.

## CONTINUING EDUCATION IS FOR EVERYMAN

At *all* of the Kellogg Foundation-assisted centers, as at the Universities of Chicago, Nebraska and Oklahoma, conferences and institutes of state, national, and international significance provide visible and vital use of the center's facilities and of the University faculties to communicate the most recent research findings to receptive practitioners. Michigan State University's "Kellogg Center," for example, has developed more than 1000 advanced seminars for such organizations as the National Science Foundation, the American Institute of Electrical Engineers, the American Mathematical Society, the National Council on Crime and Delinquency, and the American Institute of Biological Sciences.

But Continuing Education is designed to utilize all the resources of great universities to the benefit of all who may find them useful. Thus on a cold blustery day, as winter slowed traffic on the highways of Michigan, Tom

Boardman's five-year-old station wagon nudged into a snowbank edging a parking lot on the campus of Michigan State University in East Lansing. Boardman was thirty-six years old. Born in the Depression, he had graduated from high school at the beginning of the post-World War II boom, gone to work on an assembly line job in Detroit, married, sired two youngsters, a boy and a girl, and had done quite well over the years, apparently satisfied with a reasonably regular paycheck, his small subdivision home, poker on Thursday night with the boys, weekend hunting and fishing in season, and a camping trip during summer vacation. He had never before been on a university campus.

He wrestled his heavy suitcase from the back of the station wagon and

Arriving at a Continuing Education Center.

slogged through the coating of fresh snow on the ice of the parking lot toward the front entrance of an imposing seven-story building that rose near a bank of the iced-over Red Cedar River on Michigan State University's campus. Brightly sweatered and warmly parkaed youngsters in their late teens and early twenties whipped confidently past and Boardman felt the weight of his years heavier than his suitcase. The campus seemed an alien place, and the snatches of student conversation he heard were unintelligible. Boardman hesitated. He thought of giving the whole thing up, of leaving this place where he didn't belong, this institution of higher learning. But he'd come this far and he wasn't turning back now. He went on up the walk toward the big glass doors and the sign, "Kellogg Center for Continuing Education."

Boardman's tensions lessened because the glass doors provided a portal from the seemingly alien world of the college student to his familiar world of the adult traveler. He was in what appeared to be a hotel lobby. On his right was the registration desk; extending farther beyond the desk were lounge chairs and settees arranged in conversational groupings and masked from the corridor by planters and some unobtrusive structural columns; to his left was a dining room and, straight ahead, elevators. There wasn't a college boy in sight except the uniformed young man picking up another guest's luggage to show him to his room. The people occupying the lounge chairs were mature, some even gray.

Boardman set his suitcase down in front of the desk. "I'm Robert Boardman," he said. "I'm here for the Resort Owner's Seminar."

## SEMINARS MEET REAL NEEDS OF REAL PEOPLE

Boardman was one of sixty-four Michigan motel and resort owners and managers who attended that particular seminar. For Boardman, this first visit to a college campus was particularly important. After he turned thirty, life on the production line had just not been enough. He had foregone a new car every two years and had cut a little here and saved a little there until he had enough cached away for a down-payment on a small lake resort in the heart of his favorite Upper Michigan hunting and fishing country. But operating a resort is more than just owning a few cabins and boards in a scenic spot. It is a business, and a highly specialized, rather precarious business, particularly for someone like Boardman with no background or experience in such essentials as budgeting, purchasing, personnel selection and management, food preparation, housekeeping, publicity and promotion—just a few of the concerns of the modern resort owner and operator. Happily, the agent who had negotiated Boardman's purchase of the resort had told him of the Resort Owner's Seminar sponsored by the College of

Business and the Continuing Education Service of Michigan State University at the Kellogg Center for Continuing Education on the East Lansing campus. Because of the Center and its Seminar for Resort Owners, Boardman would be launching his new career with at least a better chance for success than he would have had if these educational tools had not been available to him.

On the same day that Boardman slogged through Michigan's snow toward the entrance to Kellogg Center, a nattily dressed, blue-eyed, blond young man stood in line behind a short-sleeved, middle-aged Negro in the lobby of the Georgia Center for Continuing Education in Athens, Georgia.

"Is this where the Poultry Grower's Conference is being held?" the Negro asked.

"It probably is," the young man said. "I'm here for the Georgia Legislators' Institute, but I know there's usually more than one meeting at a time going on in the Georgia Center."

The Negro, Hank Adams, operator of a small Georgia poultry farm in the same county in which his grandfather had been a slave, sat down to dinner that night with a group that included the Dean of the University's

The first order of business is registration for a room.

College of Agriculture, the regional manager of one of the country's largest milling companies, and operators of poultry farms whose volumes were in the hundred thousands. Also present were operators of small farms similar to his own.

The nattily dressed Courtland Stone, a newly elected member of the Georgia Legislature, joined more than two hundred other legislators in a two-day session designed to orient statehouse novices and to assist in the improvement of legislative procedures. Out of the sessions emerged a proposal for a complete revision of the Georgia rules of procedure, and small committees continued to meet at the Georgia Center during the winter and spring developing a document which was adopted by the Legislature at its next session.

## CONTINUING EDUCATION SERVES SPECIAL GROUPS

As the winter turned towards spring, a new Center for Continuing Education was dedicated on the campus of Notre Dame University, South Bend, Indiana. The week-long dedicatory event was an international conference

The foyer of the relatively new Center at Notre Dame University.

A theological conference at the Notre Dame Center.

on "Theological Issues of Vatican II." Some sixty-five distinguished church and lay leaders formed the conference panel carrying on the discussions in an auditorium seating four hundred; their deliberations were made available to more than a thousand persons in other locations through built-in electronic facilities, including simultaneous translation of the several languages used, with all proceedings transmitted via closed-circuit television to distant auditoriums. The theological conference at the Notre Dame Center was followed by an Executive-Management Seminar for the Civil Service Commission and a sales seminar for the Bendix Corporation; during the next month a Symposium on Academic Freedom and an International Conference on Marx and the Western World, together involving more than three hundred participants, demonstrated the potential of the Center's emphasis on humanistic and philosophical studies.

Across the Atlantic in England, twenty-four adult educators from the United States gathered at the newly enlarged and remodeled Rewley House, residential center for the Continuing Education program carried on by the Delegacy for Extra-Mural Studies of Oxford University. With them were other adult educators from Canada, Hong Kong, Singapore and England, Wales and Scotland, vanguard of many similar groups who would be journeying to Oxford to discuss twentieth century problems in surroundings dating back to the beginning of modern education.

11

In common with most of the Continuing Education Centers, Oxford's Rewley House is host to many international conferees.

While conferences ranging from poultry raising to international adult education were taking place in facilities specifically designed for Continuing Education, the six New England states were joining together to lay plans for still another facility—the New England Center for Continuing Education, to be located on the campus of the University of New Hampshire but designed to serve and to be administered by the state universities of the New England region and to focus its program effort on the problems unique to the North Atlantic area. Columbia University planned to crown its new eleven-story School of International Affairs building with an International Center for Continuing Education floor designed specifically for conferences of leaders in international affairs and international affairs education, the Center being electronically equipped to provide for immediate and wide dissemination of deliberations taking place there through radio, television, and publication.

In April of 1968 a grant of $3 million was made by the Foundation to the California State Polytechnic College to assist in establishing physical facilities and developing the program during the first five years of a "Kellogg West" residential center for Continuing Education on a campus near Pomona, California. This campus was once the Arabian Horse Ranch of W. K. Kellogg. There the newest Center will focus upon occupational-professional objectives through skills training and "learning by doing." It is singular also in that it is the first residential center for Continuing Education to be established as an integral part of a statewide system of public higher education—the 19-institution California State College System.

This was Continuing Education as conceived and practiced in ten centers financially assisted by the Kellogg Foundation, whose first venture in the special field of residential adult learning had been crystallized by the opening of the Michigan State Center in 1951, just fifteen years before. In the fifteen years that followed the idea had swept on to college and university campuses in all parts of the United States so that by 1966, in addition to the nine Kellogg Foundation-assisted centers, there were some eighty additional academic facilities devoted exclusively to residential continuing education. In addition, business, industry, church groups, labor groups—virtually all organizations concerned with the continuing education of mankind—were adapting the idea to their purposes and budgets.

## SOME QUOTATIONS BEARING UPON CONTINUING EDUCATION

"When one considers in its length and in its breadth the importance of this question of education, the broken lives, the defeated hopes, the national failures which result from the frivolous inertia with which it is treated, it is difficult to restrain within one's self a savage rage. In the conditions of modern life, the rule is absolute, the race which does not value trained intelligence is doomed. Not all your heroism, not all your social charm, not all your wit, not all your victories on land or at sea, can move back the finger of fate. Today we maintain ourselves. Tomorrow science will have moved forward yet one more step, and there will be no appeal from the judgment which will then be pronounced on the uneducated." From the *Aims of Education* by Alfred North Whitehead.

"A person who does not continue year after year to add to his knowledge and insight can never really be an educated man. In fact, just the opposite is likely to occur. Change is a law of life. Nothing remains static. Our interests either broaden or narrow. Our thoughts deepen or become ever more shallow. We grow in knowledge and perception or our minds shrink away to insignificance . . . And it is the ripe fruit of continuing education which provides the nourishment the mind needs to grow in vision." U.S. Senator William Benton.

"Sir Eric Ashby once said: 'A university degree, at least in science, should lapse after ten years unless it is refreshed.' When Ashby said this, it was generally regarded as a pleasing witticism. Many schools seem to work on the principle that once their pupils escape from their educational embrace, they are lost for good . . . Adult education should be nearly universal in its scope and attractiveness." From *Continuing Education in Theory and in Practice,* Rewley House, Oxford University, England.

"As Voltaire remarked when chatting with his fellow inmates of Elysium: 'They are, I am told, about to extend the school age in England. They will extend it to seventy, I hope." From *Socrates Asks Why* by Eric Linklater.

The Kellogg Center for Continuing Education at Michigan State University—the first of ten such centers financially assisted by the W. K. Kellogg Foundation.

## ADULT EDUCATION HAS A LONG HISTORY

Adult education itself was not a new idea. Starting with the desire to spread the Christian faith in the early eighteenth century, teachers in England and Scotland had organized evening literacy classes so that adults could be taught to read the Bible. With the advent of the nineteenth century industrial revolution, social reformers had organized mechanics' institutes and people's colleges to aid the worker in broadening his cultural horizons as well as in increasing his technical skills. In Denmark, residential folk high schools aided in bringing that small country from impoverished serfdom to affluent democracy by 1900. In the United States, Lyceum lecture series and Chautauqua tent shows spread culture from coast to coast, and the Agricultural Extension Service of the Land-Grant College system revolutionized agricultural practices through lectures, demonstrations and short courses for adults. In addition, the public schools and universities provided evening classes, conferences, institutes, and short courses on subjects ranging from hobbies to higher mathematics, although libraries and correspondence schools, private and public, made it possible for adults to study individually and at home.

But with all these opportunities for adult education, the basic concept—that one period of systematic formal education received quite early in life was enough for most individuals—continued to be the basis on which parents and pedagogues proceeded. Adult education had been viewed primarily as an opportunity for an individual to attain an educational level which, for one reason or another, he had failed to attain in his younger days.

Today, however, that concept is no longer adequate. A leading executive explained it this way:

"As viewed from the world of business, what was studied in college is yesterday's knowledge. But what will be needed for a future business career is tomorrow's knowledge. . . . No matter how much education one has, it is not enough. . . . Unless one devotes time and energy to continuing his education, he will become an educational dropout."

And as if in both rebuttal and agreement, the president of a large, mid-western university said in a commencement address, "A university is the place where tomorrow is made."

## NEW CONCEPT IS "ALL-INCLUSIVENESS"

To cope with the condition of change, to provide for the educational needs of individuals and society, a new concept was needed. As Clifford M. Hardin, Chancellor of the University of Nebraska, put it:

"A concept of all-inclusiveness is absolutely vital. It is our hope that the University can provide an effective program which will tend the needs of the youngsters entering our secondary schools, the young adult entering into the challenging world of reality, the middle-aged and their needs for vocational refresher work, and the older-age group who need not despairingly contemplate a diminution of vocational productiveness and an attenuation of those things which help us live a life."

That new concept has been called "Continuing Education." Implicit in the term is the idea that education is now a lifelong process and that there must be both opportunity and motivation for an individual to increase his knowledge and skills through periodic study as an adult whether he was a high school drop-out, a high school graduate, or a person with college training or a graduate degree. Initially, both the name "Continuing Education" and the concept in action have been embodied most dramatically in those university-based centers for Continuing Education which have been assisted financially by the Kellogg Foundation in the period from 1951 to 1968. It is in these centers and others stimulated by them on campuses throughout the United States, and now in England, in which the Joe Boardmans—seeking information to help them make a successful transition from one vocation to another, and the Hank Adamses, seeking to increase their knowledge and skill in present vocations—may join with others of like needs to search out solutions. Along with professional men, physicians, lawyers, engineers, teachers, they strive to keep abreast of new developments in their fields, and with public officials, scientists and statesmen, search for new paths to peace, prosperity and personal fulfillment. All may come to deliberate in a functionally created environment utilizing the resources of a great university, supplemented where appropriate by the additional resources of business, industry, church and state, and administered by specially trained staffs. In these centers, Continuing Education is taking shape as a mid-Twentieth Century design for the unending education of mankind.

CHAPTER 2

# The Genesis of the Idea: How the Ten Centers Were Conceived

Winston Churchill once said, "We shape our structures and they forever after shape us." To the builder of a center for Continuing Education, this statement is a warning and a challenge. It is unlikely, however, that when officials of the Kellogg Foundation and Michigan State College began in 1944 to discuss special facilities for an adult Rural Life Institute that they had any thought of fashioning a structure which would, in turn, shape not only their participation in adult education for many years to come but would also help shape the adult education participation of universities and colleges—and, indeed, of business, industry, and other agencies—in the United States, Canada and England. Yet that is what happened.

The genesis of the idea was uncomplicated and logical. Michigan State College, a Land-Grant institution, later renamed Michigan State University, had long been involved in providing short courses for its rural constituency, one effort being a residential on-campus short course for farm youth which had been financed with assistance from the Kellogg Foundation since 1938. The institute had been very successful, and John A. Hannah, president of the college, wanted not only to continue it but also to expand it.

## KELLOGG FOUNDATION LONG INVOLVED IN ADULT EDUCATION

In addition to the Farm Youth Institute, the Kellogg Foundation had participated in a wide variety of adult education activities growing out of its initial concern to provide for the well-being of children. From the first, the trustees of the Foundation had decided to concentrate on the application of knowledge rather than on research or relief. But the application of knowledge for the welfare of children, through other than direct relief, was not a simple matter. Parents, teachers, doctors, dentists, social workers—the people who would have to apply the knowledge—did not know what knowledge was available and, therefore, could not translate it into action programs for the welfare of children. Needed was an adult education program for

17

all of the people in the community who had anything to do with health, education, recreation or welfare, so that they could identify their problems, locate resources, talk with others who had solved similar problems, and develop their own answers cooperatively. The Foundation focused on the seven-county rural area around Battle Creek, Michigan, home of W. K. Kellogg and his cereals factory, and decided to develop the area as a kind of gigantic laboratory. The experiment became known as the Michigan Community Health Project.

One of the first adult education efforts of the Foundation was a one-day seminar for the dentists of two counties, held in Battle Creek in 1933. Luncheon was followed by a lecture and demonstration of new techniques of children's dentistry, and after dinner there was a "table clinic and round-table discussion" on the economics of children's dentistry. All the dentists from one county and all but two from the second attended the meeting.

Since at the time no dental school had a postgraduate course in children's dentistry, the Foundation worked with Northwestern University Dental School and Chicago College of Dental Surgery of Loyola University to develop such a course. Only twelve dentists at a time could attend the two-week session, but within twelve months every dentist in the area had taken the course.

The same year, the Foundation sponsored the attendance of twenty-four doctors at short-term postgraduate medical courses. Evaluating this activity, the Foundation medical director wrote: "Money can be expended to no better advantage in conducting a program of preventive medicine than by first preparing the medical man in the local field to do the work."

FOUNDATION CAMPS

To give direct assistance to children from broken homes, children with special physical needs, and children who seemed destined to become delinquent, the Foundation constructed three year-round camps whose purpose was "the training of youngsters in practical preparation for life and citizenship in a democracy." As an experiment, when the camps were not occupied by children, the Foundation staff invited three different groups of teachers to the Foundation camp for week-end institutes. Later in the year, Foundation personnel visiting rural schools noted a marked difference in the attitude of the teachers who had attended the encampments from those who had not. The Director of Health Education wrote in her annual report that as a result of this encampment, when there had been time to go into detail about the Foundation health work, "it seems very conservative to state that the program in the counties, urban areas included, was speeded up one year."

Other facets of the Foundation's program picked up the encampment technique. One hundred fifty probate judges, probation officers, welfare agents, and others held a conference at Clear Lake Camp under the auspices of the Foundation and in cooperation with the State Welfare Department. Soon recreational supervisors, librarians, library trustees, service committees, and others held short-term residential courses as part of their training program in the Michigan Community Health Project, and a week-long camp for one hundred and twenty-five mothers and about twenty-five infants was held in 1938. Of this camp a Foundation staff member wrote:

"For many of the mothers, all of them farmers' wives, it was the first vacation they had ever had. It was the first time they had ever been camping. It was the first time most of them had ever sat down to a meal which they hadn't either planned, prepared, or helped to prepare. It was the first time they had really been free of responsibility (the nurses took care of all the babies, demonstrating modern methods in child care). In this setting of freedom and relaxation the staff had planned a leisurely program of instruction which dovetailed with the life activities of the camp; the instruction in foods was related to the meals they ate and the lessons in child care were demonstrated on their own children by the nurses."

Although W. K. Kellogg, then active in the affairs of the Foundation, never changed his particular desire "to lighten the burdens of children, to set their feet on surer paths to health and happiness," he saw that in many instances the problems of youth were so involved with those of adults that only through programs with adults could youth best be served.

## FARM YOUTH PROGRAM

A Farm Youth Program was initiated in the fall of 1938 when Michigan State College arranged for two groups of farm youth to take an eight-week course in agriculture, farm economics, personal hygiene, and public health. Thirty boys and thirty girls comprised each group, which, in addition to taking more formal courses, participated in social and leadership development activities.

The individualizing of this program and its concern with other than purely vocational problems was of particular interest to the Foundation. A description of the plan was included in the 1943-1944 Foundation Report:

"Group meetings, parties, meeting boys and girls, living with others, public speaking and new experiences all lead to a better understanding of the ways of life for these young people. . . . It is evident that the course . . . has contributed toward increasing the social and economic efficiency of the individual."

Two years later, the farm youth course had become so popular that 220 students participated. A review of the program indicated that "The leadership training phase . . . functioned exceedingly well," but there was one flaw in the operation. The students in this program were quartered in regular dormitories with students taking other courses. The reviewer commented:

"It would help considerably in intensifying the effectiveness of this part of the course for the scholarship group if adequate and efficient dormitory and dining facilities were available for *all* short course students. . . . Building facilities adequate for the group could aid considerably in improving the program."

Since the Farm Youth Institute had proved successful over a period of time, Emory W. Morris, head of the Foundation, was hopeful of phasing out the Foundation's direct participation in that single activity so that it could finance similar programs elsewhere.

## CHILDREN'S CLASSROOMS DON'T FIT ADULTS

Despite his desire to phase the Foundation out of the program, Dr. Morris listened with a sympathetic ear when President Hannah suggested a special facility for developing an adult Rural Life institute. Morris recalled sending one hundred rural women to the Merrill-Palmer school in Detroit for a child development course. The course had been excellent, but finding suitable facilities had involved much trouble. The same thing had been true when the Foundation underwrote the expenses of a group of school trustees to attend institutes on school problems at the University of Chicago and Northwestern University, and when, similarly, physicians, dentists and public health nurses were transported to other educational sites.

The classrooms had been equipped for children or young people, not adults, and the rural women, the school trustees and the professional people had wedged uncomfortably into the bolted-to-the-floor desks and the hard, straight-backed, tablet-arm chairs which were the classroom staples of schools and colleges. In addition, meeting rooms were changed because of previously-scheduled regular classes, participants got lost in the labryinth of corridors, time was wasted traveling between dormitories or hotels and classrooms, and, once out of the educational environment, participants sometimes let shopping trips and sight-seeing take precedence over returning to study.

The utilization of public facilities had not been much better. Although hotels were equipped with adult-sized furniture, it was seldom designed for educational purposes. Lighting was poor, portable blackboards were unstable, and again, previous scheduling of facilities caused constant changes of room assignments.

## MULTIPURPOSE BUILDING CONCEIVED

Conversations continued between Michigan State and the Foundation. By 1945 Hannah was saying:

"I have a notion that we might kill two or three birds with one stone by tying together a building project devoted to continuing education, with classrooms and facilities for handling the conferences and very short courses, providing housing and feeding facilities, and at the same time providing facilities for teaching courses in hotel administration."

The last idea had not crept in by accident. For many years the Hotel Association of Michigan had been urging Michigan State College to develop an inn-on-the-campus as a laboratory for its hotel administration students, and the hotel group had backed up its urging with a pledge of at least one hundred thousand dollars to help make the inn a reality.

Some reservations were expressed about the proposal because it was believed that the program should be the dominant concern and it appeared that at this stage the program had not been nearly as well conceived as the facility itself. "It should not be a traditional classroom building but should make use of the best things we know in adult education practices."

## MINNESOTA CENTER VISITED

One of the prototypes to which the College and Foundation turned was the University of Minnesota Center for Continuation Study, which had been built in 1936 with the assistance of P.W.A. funds. The Minnesota Center, conceived by the University's President, Lotus D. Coffman, was the first specially designed campus facility for residential continuation education. The Minnesota director warned that one should not think small in designing such a facility. Despite the Center's three floors devoted exclusively to continuation study, program people at Minnesota felt the need for more dining rooms, more conference alcoves on the dormitory floors, more conference and seminar rooms, more suites, more single rooms with bath, and a larger auditorium.

As a result of their conversations and study, Michigan State, the Hotel Association and the Foundation agreed to go ahead with the project, and on September 19, 1945, the Foundation board of trustees allocated one million dollars for the Center.

Much planning and many frustrations and changes lay between the original grant and the grand opening of the Kellogg Center at Michigan State University on September 23, 1951, but the big idea was in the wind, and alert minds were perceptive enough to catch it. For instance, November 29, 1945, the *Nashville Tennessean* editorialized: "The Foundation has launched another pioneering effort of probably even greater significance than some of its previous activities." The newspaper referred to the Continuing Education Center as a "people's college," and suggested that "educators of the region should invite the attention of the Kellogg Foundation." President Omer C. Aderhold of the University of Georgia, whose conference director had been hoping to have an old dormitory remodelled for an adult conference center, was an early negotiator with the Foundation.

The Michigan State idea had grown from a relatively limited concept to plans for a massive and multi-purpose structure. Aderhold's Georgia Center was built on a big idea from the start—not just a conference center with eating and sleeping accommodations as useful adjuncts, but a modern adult learning center to include in addition to the living and learning wings, "a full-fledged television station, a radio broadcasting station, and a studio for the production of twenty full-length documentary films annually." The idea was that "the synchronized use of films, television and radio would prolong the opportunity for learning both prior to and after the visit of groups to the campus." Hugh Masters became its first director when the Georgia

At the Georgia Center, the synchronized use of television, radio, and films prolongs the opportunity for learning both prior to and after visits to the campus.

Center opened in 1956. Masters was still director a decade later and could say with some pride, "This Center was conceived, designed and functions to do what it does." And what the Georgia Center does, according to its staff, is demonstrate the team concept of Continuing Education in which the building itself, and all of its functions are part of the teaching-learning team. And one official said, standing in the spacious and inviting lobby for the first time at the dedication ceremonies, "This building will make every Georgian put on a clean shirt."

A grant of $1,690,000 for construction and $454,000 for program support was made by the Foundation to the University of Georgia in 1953. In the years following, the Foundation was deluged with requests for similar facilities, so the Trustees asked the staff to make a careful review of the Foundation's participation in Continuing Education for the Trustees' guidance in considering these requests. A document which was submitted to the Trustees in 1957 has since become known as the "Fifteen Criteria" and has had great influence on the development of continuing education centers. Because of its significance, most of the document is included here:

## THE FIFTEEN CRITERIA

Continuing Education is a term describing a new concept of education. This term, as now interpreted, was first used twelve years ago when it became necessary to give a title or name to the program in adult education which was being planned at Michigan State University. The Foundation and University officials agreed then that the new concept of education was best described by the word "continuing."

For the most part, American efforts at education and training had been, up to that time, concerned with . . . equipping *new* people. . . . The young man who had graduated in medicine or engineering or agriculture, or who had completed a terminal curriculum in electricity or carpentry or hotel management was presumed to be sufficiently prepared to serve for the remainder of his active years with but casual attention to additional training. . . . Adult education twelve years ago was, when viewed in the overall, sporadic, superficial, and usually consisted of an unrelated series of educational activities promoted by well-meaning, but unstable agencies.

But in 1945 when the Kellogg Foundation decided to aid Michigan State University in demonstrating a concept of education to be known as "Continuing Education," a new movement was inaugurated—a movement that was destined to give to adult education a new emphasis, a new mission. The Foundation knew at that time, because of its experience with projects that emphasized self-help, that the application of knowledge usually lagged far behind the discovery of truth. The Foundation knew from real experience that the crying need was for an education that continued after formal schooling was over, after the diploma or certificate was awarded.

Now as we review the situation twelve years later, as we take a look at the development of Continuing Education at Michigan State University, at the University of Georgia . . . and in other institutions where more specialized programs of Continuing Education for certain professional groups have been developed with Foundation support, we see clearly that the confidence which the Foundation expressed through the granting of funds was indeed justified. . . .

Many letters and personal messages have been received from persons who have visited the Continuing Education Centers or who have read reports about them. These many inquiries concerning aid reveal clearly the great impact which the Foundation-supported projects have made upon adult education. They contain plans which call for the use of institutional resources along with Foundation aid. Because of the intense interest, there apparently exists today an unusual opportunity to expand further this new concept of education. And with rising construction costs, timing becomes an important factor.

The peculiar characteristics of Continuing Education demand a special type of building which combines in one structure conference rooms, display space, auditoriums, communication systems, duplicating and distributing equipment, over-night rooming quarters and dining facilities. This type of structure is unique in American architecture. *In fact, the facility for Continuing Education at Michigan State University will undoubtedly be referred to by historians as the beginning of an entirely new type of educational facility.* The demonstrations which we have supported in Continuing Education reveal such willingness and enthusiasm on the part of adults to participate that operational budgets, after a few years of subsidy, have not been difficult to maintain on a self-supporting basis or with only minor contributions from other sources. This characteristic of the program—the willingness of the participants to pay all, or nearly all, of the operational expenses for their conference—is another important reason why this new concept of education should be expanded.

From the considerations which we have given to the new proposals and to the various inquiries, we have formulated a list of fifteen criteria which seem to us to be important as we make decisions with respect to specific commitments. The criteria are:

1. Unique features of proposed program (as compared with MSU and the University of Georgia).

   A tentative conclusion which we have reached is that careful consideration should be given to at least one *private* university. This university would become a demonstration to determine what would be the clientele in Continuing Education for a private university, what service areas could be rendered by this type of institution, and what are the chances for such a program in such an institution being self-supporting. Some of the proposals which we have from *publicly supported* institutions describe some unique features, such as the inclusion of a special section of the building for . . . out-of-school youth who have not gone beyond high school . . . and including in the program some new professional groups such as those related to the health field.

2. Status of planning—extent to which specific plans have been formulated.

   This criterion is used to determine whether or not the institution has seriously considered this new concept of education. Some institutions have an opportunistic approach, seeming to be just interested in getting in on a new movement if funds are available, while other institutions reveal a genuine interest backed up by specific plans.

3. Extent and quality of involvement of staff in the planning—evidence of genuine acceptance of this concept of education.

At the heart of this new movement in education is the continuing involvement of the so-called regular members of the university staff in the continuing education activities.

In fact, Continuing Education, as we define the term, serves as a major channel through which the regular faculty member makes application very quickly of his research findings. If a proposal has been planned by only a small specialized staff, a genuine Continuing Education Center is not likely to be achieved.

4. Evaluation procedures included in plan; research on adult education and educative process included in plan; dissemination of results included in plan.

We have had sufficient experience in this new field of education now to justify a careful evaluation to answers of such questions as: What activities are really producing the desired results? What activities, which seem effective, have really very little educative value? What type of pre-conference and post-conference activities are effective? What is the desirable length of a conference? What activities should be self-supporting and under what conditions? What instructional materials are needed to make the learning process more effective? What are the efficient ways to use the mass media of communication? As we review the plan of evaluation, we expect to learn of the institution's record with respect to its interest in the field of adult education—to learn whether or not significant research has been conducted. Since a major reason for our supporting additional projects is our desire to have this new movement in education expanded, we shall be interested in the plans which are presented for the dissemination of the results obtained.

5. Training programs for professional leaders in the field of adult education as a part of plan.

There is now a shortage of trained professional leaders in the field of adult education. . . . Continuing Education centers are ideal for the giving of work experience to students who are enrolled in curriculums for the preparation of adult education leaders.

6. Recognition in plans of necessity for pre- and post-conference experiences—*continuing* Continuing Education.

A conference can be, of course, an isolated educational activity. If Continuing Education is to be truly *continuing,* a conference program must have a relationship to the participant's pre-conference and post-conference experiences.

7. Space planning.

A study of the planning which has taken place with respect to space frequently reveals whether or not the institution really has an understanding of this new concept of education. For example, some institutions make provision for a very small number of staff offices, clearly indicating that they do not understand the function of the continuing education center staff.

8. Experience to date in conducting adult education activities.

An institution which has had no experience in conducting adult education activities may not be ready to accept the responsibilities for a major program which a Continuing Education facility makes possible. Perhaps such an institution should first continue a more limited program.

9. Ability of the leadership designated for the program.

A wonderful physical facility does not, of course, guarantee a superior program. The facility makes possible a superior program when there is a *superior* staff.

10. Geographic location: (a) State coverage, (b) Regional coverage, (c) National coverage, and (d) International coverage.

11. Professions and other groups represented in institution's program.

Because institutions train for different professions, some of them present unique opportunities to explore the possibilities of continuing education. We shall be interested in extending demonstrations in continuing education to some new professional and leadership groups.

12. Desirability and cost of site or sites.

Unless the site is carefully chosen, the entire program may be jeopardized. It is especially important to provide a large amount of parking space.

13. Stability of central administration of the institution.

Although we cannot expect individual leaders in an institution to remain indefinitely in their present positions, we should be assured of a stable administration which can be depended upon even though administrative leaders may change.

14. Analysis of necessary financing—cost of center, possibilities of matching Foundation funds; program budget, amount requested from Foundation; number of years.

Sometimes the real test of an institution's interest is its willingness or unwillingness to match Foundation funds or to assume responsibility for the operation budget.

15. Opportunity for the observation and use of the new facility to make contributions to the local community's standard of living—particularly to the understanding of the use of color, of new kinds of building materials, of modern furnishings and local flora.

The Centers at Michigan State University and at the University of Georgia are exerting a postive influence in their local communities. This influence is for a higher standard of living. Local citizens take pride in having these centers in their community; they observe the artistic effects of color combinations, of various types of construction and of placement and use of modern furnishings. It seems obvious that such observations will affect the attitudes of local citizens as these citizens enjoy the use of the facilities.

The "Fifteen Criteria" served as guides for the development of many proposals for Continuing Education centers in addition to the ten founded in part by the Foundation. (Fifty-three such proposals were received between 1957 and 1961.) A number of proposals not accepted by the Foundation were so compelling to their sponsors that they sought other means of financing and the centers were brought into being.

In the genesis of the idea, the development of the "Fifteen Criteria" has significance comparable to the building of the pilot centers, and the criteria remain the most useful single guide for educators contemplating the construction of a Continuing Education center.

## NEBRASKA CENTER PLANNED

One of the proposals on the desk of Maurice Seay, Foundation Educational Director, as he was working with the rest of the staff and the organization's Education advisors to develop the "Fifteen Criteria," was from the University of Nebraska whose Chancellor, Clifford Hardin, had been Dean of Agriculture at Michigan State. Hardin knew what he wanted in a Continuing Education facility. He and Knute Broady—Director of General Extension and the first Director of the Nebraska Center—conceived of a plan designed to sustain what they called an "all-inclusive program" to serve the Continuing Education needs of youth as well as adults, and to meet the requirements of farm, town and gown. A key part of the structure and program was to be the Hall of Youth, where the idea of "Continuing Education" could be built into the secondary school life of young people facing the decision of whether to stay on the farm by developing new atti-

The Nebraska Center for Continuing Education, with the taller adult section connected by a central kitchen and service arcade with a three-story "Hall of Nebraska Youth."

tudes and practices appropriate to the automating Twentieth Century, or to migrate to the city and adapt to urban industrial ways. To develop the Hall of Youth idea, Hardin and Broady called on Otto Hoiberg, whose father had been director of two American Danish folk high schools, and the Hall of Youth was conceived of as combining some of the advantages of the Danish institution with the resources of a great American university: it would be a place where young adults could come for specific advice and assistance in making life decisions and in preparing themselves to implement their choices.

## OKLAHOMA ENVISIONS "COMMUNITY IN MINIATURE"

Shortly after World War II Thurman White, Dean of Extension at the University of Oklahoma, found himself operating an adult education program in a group of hastily built and rapidly abandoned wooden navy barracks. These were not only entirely unsuited to both the personal and educational housing needs of his adult students, but were also located some distance from the main university campus and had been declared dangerous fire traps. Clearly, new quarters were essential if White was to develop a viable and lasting program. In Oklahoma's rurally dominated legislature, however, the average lawmaker equated "Extension" with the Agricultural College which was part of the Land-Grant Oklahoma State University, not the University of Oklahoma, White's base of operations. So White turned to the Kellogg Foundation with his idea of a complex of buildings which would constitute a "community in miniature" to serve the continuing education needs of the whole Southwest.

White's idea was to provide for a coming-together and a "withdrawal" in every aspect of the Center's design and operation. Participants were to come together as a group on the University campus for the period of their study; they would withdraw to smaller meeting rooms for discussion following the large meeting; and they would return to the main forum for sharing their deliberations as a large group at periodic intervals during the sessions. One other major innovation was also part of White's plan: a special degree for adults which would be achieved by a combination of independent study in the individual's home environment and periodic residential study sessions

---

$\longrightarrow$

Unlike the other Foundation-assisted facilities, the Oklahoma Center consists of a complex of relatively small buildings instead of a single large structure: (*a*) is of the hexagonal Forum Building of the Center, having 20 conference rooms plus a "Forum Room" seating 525 people; (*b*) shows the Commons Restaurant having 3 dining rooms, each with a seating capacity of 200, to the right is The Hall of Advanced Studies, having meeting rooms and living areas; (*c*) is of "Sooner House," a 3-story dormitory with a capacity of 152 persons; (*d*) pictures one of ten duplex cottages which will hold a maximum of twenty families or eighty persons.

on-campus with a group of fellow adult degree-seekers. As President Cross pointed out, the community concept and the University resources "would facilitate the blending of occupational and special learnings with general and liberal education." Another factor President Cross emphasized for the selection of Oklahoma as a Continuing Education center site was, as he put it, "As of right now, we present the only opportunity for professional and scientific people of mixed races to meet together in this part of the nation."

## CHICAGO PROPOSES NATIONAL CENTER

At the University of Chicago, Chancellor Laurence Kimpton and Professor Cyril O. Houle conceived of a Center which would be the gathering place for national leaders in many fields in the appropriate setting provided by the city, a national transportation and communications crossroad. At the Chicago Center the object would be to "carry on Continuing Education activities for people who in turn would be carrying on Continuing Education activities for those who are to apply the results of research."

Because they believed that the informal conversations outside the meeting rooms were as important to the learning process as the more formal sessions at the conference table, Kimpton and Houle worked into their concept meeting rooms surrounded by living quarters so that participants could move easily and without interruption from the formal conference situation to the informal conversational phase and back again.

The first director of the new Center said, "Thinking will be much more continuous if conferees don't have to head for taxis and hotels when the sessions break up." He pointed out that guest rooms would accommodate two hundred. "With that number involved," he said, "many arguments can be pursued through dinner and into the night." Edward D. Stone, the famous architect who was to design the graceful Center which grew beside Chicago's Midway, said of the site that it was "fantastically beautiful" and added, "Practically the whole history of architecture is written there on the campus." Stone said:

"I look forward to the challenge of combining efficient hotel facilities with education facilities in a university atmosphere. The very idea of the Continuing Education Center intrigues me, and I'm encouraged by the idea that we don't stop learning. I find that for a busy professional most of your life is used up getting on with the job. You just can't take time out for reading and meditation and preparation for a formal attack on new problems, but when you sit down with people, each one stimulates and encourages the other. In a few hours, you will have the chance to accumulate a great deal of knowledge. The Center for Continuing Education strikes me in this way: it is the place that busy people can learn a lot in a short while."

The Chicago Center for Continuing Education, designed by Edward Durrell Stone and on the University of Chicago South Campus.

Integral to the proposal submitted by Kimpton and Houle was a studies and training program involving graduate study in adult education combined with internships in the development and coordination of Center programs and a number of research studies in various phases of Center-related continuing education.

OXFORD CENTRE REMODELED FOR CONTINUING EDUCATION

Although the five original Kellogg Foundation-assisted centers in the United States were new structures and large ones, designed to accommodate several hundred people in residence and a thousand or more in some of the auditoriums, the sixth Kellogg-assisted center at Oxford University in England was different. Frank Jessup, secretary of the Delegacy for Extra-Mural Studies, under whose direction the Center was conceived, put it this way:

*"In typical English fashion we have chosen to adapt century-old buildings rather than tear them down and erect new; and certainly in typical Oxford fashion the Centre is planned on a domestic, intimate scale, with accommodation for about fifty resident students (mostly in double study-bedrooms) and a dining room and kitchen able to cater for about seventy. The social heart of the center is the common room, shared by students and faculty; and perhaps it is there, in fact, that the richest educational experience occurs."*

The four-fold purpose of the center is (a) to enable the University the better to make its contribution toward the evolution of the good society; (b) to form a channel of communication whereby information about new discoveries and current research could be passed rapidly to men and women in industry, commerce, and the public services for whose work the information was relevant and important; (c) to help the educationally disadvantaged; and (d) to strengthen internationalism in adult education.

Among the devices proposed to accomplish these purposes is the idea of strengthening existing programs by week-end courses for students taking three-year tutorial classes, permitting a close study in a communal environment of part of the class curriculum; and week-end courses, linked together to form a progressive series, for students who because of their rural situation or vocational exigencies could not attend ordinary tutorial or sessional classes. Mr. Jessup wrote:

*"Residential programs permit studying in depth, total commitment freed from extraneous distractions, and the educative potential that is inherent in face-to-face situations. The whole Oxford tradition is indeed based on the value of a residential community consisting of a group of educators and educands. It is now intended to extend the tradition firmly into the field of adult education and to enlarge the opportunities for members of the faculty of the university and intelligent and interested adults to meet in circumstances conducive of standards of excellence in adult education."*

After visiting Oxford, Dr. Seay of the Foundation wrote: "The conclusion I reach is that adult education is clearly recognized as an important University role, that the architect and the staff have planned well the renovation and the new facility, that Oxford is very much aware of current problems in its community, in its country, and in the world, and that there is a real desire to relate education to many needs. Obviously the 'Ivy Tower' concept does not prevail at this University in spite of its age and tradition. I believe this Center for Continuing Education to be established at Oxford University can be tremendously successful, not only as a demonstration in England but also as an influence in promoting this concept of education in other countries."

The Oxford proposal was approved by the Foundation in the summer of 1963, and, in July, Jessup wrote to say how happy the Oxonians were. At the end of what he termed "a business and humdrum letter," Jessup said:

*"I cannot end it without saying how excited I feel at the possibilities which the residential Center now opens out for us, and particularly the possibilities for cooperation with adult educators in North America.*

*"Adult education in England has a long and fine history and great achievement to its credit. It possesses certain qualities which must at all cost be preserved. But the very fact that it has been a successful achievement makes it the more necessary that we should not allow ourselves to become stuck in a groove or to allow our one good custom to corrupt the world.*

*"I am sure we shall gain a great deal from contact with our friends in adult education in North America, not necessarily by copying their methods, because systems of adult education are not in general suitable for export, but by looking at our own problems afresh and in the light of your experience.*

*"Somehow, I think it is significant that I should be writing to you in these terms on the Fourth of July."*

## NOTRE DAME DEVELOPS A PHILOSOPHIC CONFERENCE CENTER

All the Centers up to this point had been conceived of as residential as well as educational. At the University of Notre Dame, a private Roman Catholic institution for men, there already existed the Morris Inn, a well-appointed hotel for campus visitors and conference participants. However, the Reverend Theodore M. Hesburgh, president of the University, felt the need for a conference facility to be used in conjunction with the Inn. On February 28, 1962, he wrote to the Kellogg Foundation. "The University in recent years has been entering a new era which might best be described as a work of mediation between the University and the world at large," he said. "What is unique about the University of Notre Dame is that it is generally recognized as the outstanding Catholic University in this country, if not in the whole world. Such a position brings with it added responsibilities. Simply because we are a Catholic University, we have no desire to be a ghetto."

Hesburgh saw the Continuing Education Center as almost in total an experimental program. Several specifics included the following:

1. What are the uses and opportunities for educational television in Continuing Education?

2. Can you develop a significant program of counseling and guidance for those interested in continuing their education?

3. What is the best means for extending Continuing Education to Notre Dame alumi and to Notre Dame friends?

4. What is the best way to proceed in interfaith and intercultural seminars and conferences?

5. How can Notre Dame's Continuing Education Center make its best contribution to long-range programs in school administration? Two factors important in the proposal were the University's substantive Center for the

33

Study of Man in Contemporary Society and the fact that Notre Dame had "prominence in the area of inter-credal, inter-cooperative, and inter-group studies and projects." Among the items in the proposal were that "it would be recommended to the Dean or Director that he work on an internship arrangement with the University of Chicago so that persons studying for their doctorates in Continuing Education at Chicago would, for a period of time, assist in the operation of the Continuing Education Center at Notre Dame."

Hesburgh's concept involved a building of great flexibility, with many meeting rooms of many sizes, and an auditorium which would make possible multilingual discussion by large participating groups. Also included were "apartments"—actually quiet resting rooms—for visiting lecturers and discussion leaders who would be on campus for only a short time.

The special area of contribution at Notre Dame would, of course, be philosophical discussion. However, it was clear that the Center would serve the academic and business community in the broadest possible sense as well as contribute to denominational and ecumenical discussion.

The aforementioned centers were all built and in operation by 1966, but two more were yet to come.

## NEW ENGLAND CENTER INVOLVES SIX-STATE COOPERATION

Despite the fact that by 1966 the Kellogg Foundation believed that its contributions had assisted in the development of a comprehensive variety of Continuing Education centers and that it should phase itself out of this "business," the universities of the six New England states—Connecticut, Maine, Massachusetts, New Hampshire, Rhode Island, and Vermont—came to the Foundation with a proposal for a regional center to be located on the campus of the University of New Hampshire but to be supported and programmed by all six universities cooperatively.

The idea of developing such a regional center to pool the intellectual, cultural and economic resources of New England to serve the eleven million people in six states by grappling with regional problems and developing programs to solve them, was a compelling concept. In addition to the Center itself—on a wooded corner of the New Hampshire campus where the boulder-strewn pine and brook site would provide a Thoreau-like environment ready-made for contemplative and imaginative thinking—each university proposed to undertake a particular area of concern: Maine, to stimulate cooperative approaches to the development, conservation and effective use of New England's economic, natural, and human resources; New Hampshire, to design an interdisciplinary inter-institutional graduate program in adult

Pictured is the architects' model of the New England Center for Continuing Education (now under construction) on the campus of the University of New Hampshire. William L. Pereira and Associates are the architects.

education; Vermont, to develop programs in continuing medical education; Massachusetts, to enhance student culture and develop community colleges; Connecticut, to develop continuing education programs in the visual and performing arts; and Rhode Island, to concentrate upon education for and service to the aging.

Under the guidance of Arthur Adams, former president of the University of New Hampshire and longtime head of the American Council on Education, the New England Center began to grow through the conversion of a fraternity house to a headquarters building and the initiation of pilot programs by the cooperating schools, while architects, designers and fund raisers worked to perfect plans for major installations.

COLUMBIA UNIVERSITY PLANS
INTERNATIONAL AFFAIRS CONFERENCE CENTER

When Andrew Cordier, Dean of Columbia University's School of International Affairs (and former key member of the United Nations Secretariat, where he shared across-the-board responsibilities with both Secretary-

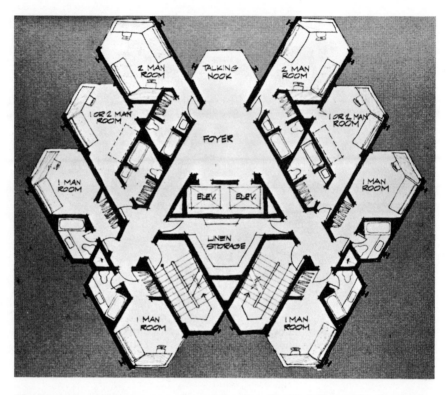

The floor plan of the tower portion of the New England Center for Continuing Education, currently being constructed on the campus of the University of New Hampshire.

Generals Dag Hammerschold and Trygvie Lie) began to plan for a fifteen-story, eighteen million dollar building to house the School's areas studies research and teaching institutes, he also conceived of a conference center as part of the building and its program. The Center would be a specially designed facility where carefully selected leaders in international affairs could gather for effective interchange of ideas and information and thus contribute to reasoned decision making at the policy level in matters of global import. "The Conference Center," Cordier said, "will be a vital feature of the new home for the School of International Affairs. The entire top floor, as well as related services and space in the rest of the building, and particularly the auditorium, will be utilized to provide this important service to the public. The Center will be equipped with audio-visual services, including television, so that highly significant programs can be brought to the attention of a larger public."

The Kellogg Foundation agreed to assist in making this part of the project a reality, so when, in the winter of 1966–1967, huge earth moving machines began to attack a vast slab of Manhattan Island bedrock undergirding one

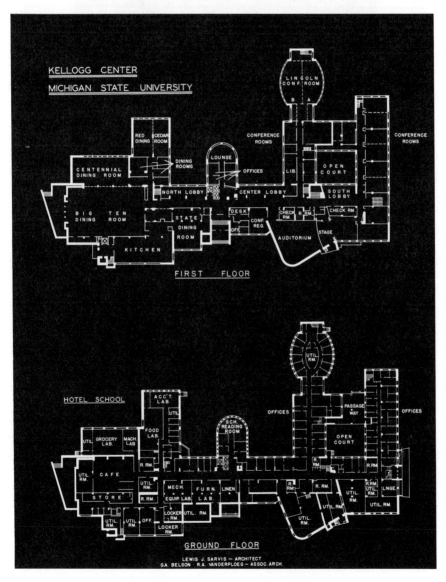

Plans of the first two floors of Kellogg Center, Michigan State University; plans of the dormitory floors above them are not shown.

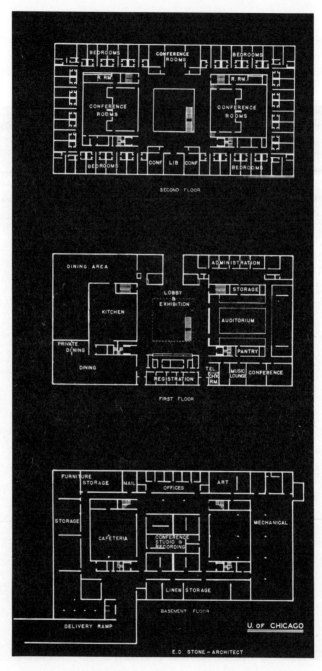

Plans of the first three floors of the Chicago Center; the plans of the dormitory floors are not shown.

38

corner of the Columbia University campus, Dean Cordier could point to the top floor on the model of the building in his office and say that there, at the crown of the building, would be Columbia University's International Center for Continuing Education.

## FROM CHILDREN'S HEALTH TO ADULT EDUCATION

Thus the desire of one man, W. K. Kellogg, to provide for the health and happiness of children had led to the development of what was hailed as a new concept of adult education, a concept that had roots in the nineteenth century Danish folk high school and that promised to have significance for twentieth century international affairs; the Kellogg goal was now to contribute not just to children but rather to the welfare of all mankind.

The genesis of the idea of Continuing Education involved a combining of the American Land-Grant college techniques of rural youth and adult education with methods designed to meet the educational needs of the urban industrial and professional populations. The investment by the Kellogg Foundation in pilot projects at Michigan State University and the University of Georgia led to the development of the previously mentioned "Fifteen

Under construction is Columbia University's fifteen-floor building to house the School of International Affairs and related Institutes. The top floor of the structure will house the Foundation-aided International Center for Continuing Education.

Criteria," on which grants for the rest of the ten Kellogg-assisted centers were made. Emphasizing uniqueness, planning, staff involvement, evaluation procedures, training programs for professional adult educators, pre- and post-conference experiences, institutional experience in adult education, leadership, involvement of professional groups, and contribution to the community's standard of living, the "Fifteen Criteria" focus attention on the fact that the essential values of Continuing Education abide in the quality of the content, leadership and participants. The Kellogg investment was more than "bricks and mortar," for speakers at the dedication ceremony of the first Center at Michigan State stressed that the Center was more than a building: it was a building to house an idea, and it was the idea that was important.

CHAPTER 3

# The Shaping of the Structures: Building the Centers for Continuing Education

It was some twenty years from the first Kellogg Foundation grant to Michigan State University for a center to house a program of broad scope, to the grant for the ninth Kellogg-assisted Continuing Education Center at Columbia University, a highly specialized facility for conferences in international affairs. In those twenty years of planning, building and operating a great deal was learned—about the initial cost and methods of raising money, about building delays, about inflation, about the necessity for careful planning and the sharing of experience, about mistakes in design and about remodeling. But most of all, Continuing Educators learned that learning, itself, was the goal, and that the building was simply part of the learning team.

When the committee exploring the possibilities of a Rural Life Institute facility at Michigan State University in 1944 submitted its proposal to the Kellogg Foundation, President Hannah had attached a note suggesting that the $1,500,000 the committee envisioned as the cost of the facility was far too much—he believed an adequate structure could be developed for from one-third to one-half that amount. Actually, the Center that was subsequently built involved a grant from the Kellogg Foundation, alone, of $1,400,000, plus an investment of approximately $1,000,000 by the University for site acquisition, connection of services, and site preparation and landscaping. And this was just the beginning, for three years after the building opened, an addition costing $790,000 was built, and a second addition four years later added another $500,000 to the cost, making a total direct outlay for the facility of $3,690,000.

Raw figures such as this, however, are both inconclusive and, in a very real sense, misleading. Time, not the architect, is the biggest spender. The cost of the same building in 1951 was some 250% more than it would have been in 1939, and costs have continued to rise since then.

41

The Center for Continuing Education at the University of Georgia.

When the initial grant was made by the Kellogg Foundation to the University of Georgia in 1953, the Foundation amount was $1,690,000 and the University contribution was $900,000. Building costs in Georgia, though, were less than in Michigan. For example, in 1949, the year construction was started at Michigan State, Atlanta figures were only 83.5% of similar costs in Chicago. By 1954, the year construction was started in Georgia, the estimated square-foot cost of the Georgia Center was $13.77 as compared with $12.96 per-square-foot cost of the Michigan State Center. (Yet if the Georgia Center had been built in 1949, the per-square-foot cost would have been only $10.83.) In Georgia, also, there was another complicating factor: air conditioning! This raised the actual per-square-foot cost to $15.04.

By 1965, when initial planning for the New England Center started, estimates were based on $30.00 per square foot (and construction has been delayed because planning figures were not realistic!).

## NOT A MINOR BUDGET ITEM

Whatever the figures, though, one thing is clear: the building of a center for Continuing Education, such as those assisted financially by the Kellogg Foundation, is not a minor budget item. The University of Nebraska Center came in at approximately $3,000,000, the University of Oklahoma facility cost more than $4,000,000, not including furnishings and equipment, and at the University of Chicago, where the proposal had envisioned a cost of $3,500,000, the initial bids were almost a half million more than budgeted, and, before construction was completed, costs were even higher.

Comfortable, modern furnishings contribute to the high cost of a residential Continuing Education facility. At the University of Georgia, a typical twin bedroom involved $1,237 in furnishings. At the University of Oklahoma, the total furnishings and equipment cost $332,268. In addition, special equipment compounds the cost. At the University of Georgia, where radio, television and motion pictures were an integral part of the plan, communications equipment alone cost $400,000, and at the University of Notre Dame the cost of the Center for Continuing Education was nearly $3,000,000,

Unlike other Foundation-aided centers, the Notre Dame Center shown in the upper of the two pictures has neither food nor housing facilities. Instead, lodging and meals are secured at the pre-existent, University-owned Morris Inn, just across the street.

despite the fact that the residential facility, Morris Inn, was already in existence and, therefore, neither food nor housing facilities were major cost items.

Of course, it is possible to develop a Continuing Education center for less than three or four million dollars. The Kellogg Foundation grant to the University of Oxford, for instance, was just $135,000. But the Oxford project consisted of remodeling existing buildings, while the other centers involved new construction, and the Centre at Oxford was designed to accommodate about fifty resident students and a maximum of seventy for dining, whereas the other Kellogg-assisted centers have ranged upward from 150 residents to more than 1000 for dining.

## EDUCATIONAL PHILOSOPHY IMPORTANT

The cost of a facility for Continuing Education, therefore, is not an absolute thing; it is a derivative several times removed from a number of

Rewley House, residential Center for Continuing Education as carried on by the Delegacy for Extra-Mural Studies of Oxford University, England, was remodeled and refurbished with Foundation funds.

fundamental decisions based on institutional educational philosophy and policy. First of all, an institution wishing to embark on a program of Continuing Education involving the least possible financial outlay can simply use existing facilities and staff and, in effect, ask both to operate on an overload basis to do a job for which they are neither trained nor equipped. The next step up is to hire specially trained staff who might be more adept at adapting existing facilities to special purposes than untrained people would be. Another step is to remodel existing facilities under the direction of a trained staff. And the final step, of course, is to create new facilities to be administered by a specially trained staff. In all cases the size of the Continuing Education population to be served would have a direct bearing on the cost of the facility; obviously a facility to serve twenty-five people could be commandeered, adapted, remodeled, or built for less than a facility to serve two hundred fifty.

But perhaps the overriding consideration in cost is the decision with regard to appropriateness and quality of the facility. If quality of program is the chief goal, special facilities and trained staff are essential. Even if adults *were* just tall children, the use of desks and other equipment designed for the education of the young would be inappropriate for the education of adults. The fact is, however, that adults are not just tall children. In addition to desks and other equipment that fit them physically, it is appropriate for adults to expect surroundings which acknowledge their adulthood. Adults in the United States today seldom—except under duress, as in the army, prison, or a hospital ward—live in dormitory situations, with more than two or three in a room and group toilet and bath facilities down the hall. Adults—other than those in certain religious orders—do not seek out hard pallets in bare cells for sleeping and contemplative study. Adults in the United States today do not seek out uncomfortable seats, thin walls, poor food, or dull meetings.

## SPECIALNESS COSTS MONEY

Appropriateness and quality in Continuing Education mandate specialness, and specialness costs money. At the University of Chicago, for example, specialness in Continuing Education started with the tradition of the institution, itself, as a great university dedicated to academic excellence. In Continuing Education, particularly, excellence was inherent in the program of graduate studies in adult education built by Professor Cyril O. Houle at the University of Chicago, among whose students were Thurman White, who became Dean at the University of Oklahoma; Allen Brown, who directed the studies and training program at the University of Nebraska; Tunis Dekker, head of University Conferences at Michigan State University;

and Chester Leathers, supervisor of conference coordinators at the University of Georgia.

The University of Chicago Center had to be something special, and Houle's concept, cast in concrete and carpeting by Edward Durrell Stone, one of the country's leading architects, was based on the idea that the architecture should contribute to a feeling of community, one of the essential elements in a good conference. In addition, the building was to be designed so that any group which used it would be made to feel that the building was suited to its particular needs: if there were one large conference, the members would feel that the building was designed for large conferences, while if there were several smaller conferences, the members of each one should feel that the building was built for their own small conference. Moreover, the Chicago Center was to be a national center involving leaders in many fields in seminars of vital importance; this fact dictated furniture and fixtures representing the finest in craftsmanship and taste, qualities seldom associated with inexpensiveness.

## GETTING THE MONEY

Getting the money has been, therefore, a major preoccupation of all those who have determined to build a center for Continuing Education. In connection with those assisted by the Kellogg Foundation, securing of the grant was merely a first step—a giant step, to be sure, and one achieved only after

The main foyer and an overhanging balcony at the Chicago Center for Continuing Education.

careful planning and presentation of a proposal indicating the unique features of the proposed program, the involvement of university-wide staff participation in planning, the designation of strong leadership based on prior experience in Continuing Education activities, and many other factors, including a clear financial commitment on the part of the institution.

At Michigan State the University accepted full responsibility for the acquisition and development of the site, although the Michigan Hotel Association agreed to underwrite at least $100,000 of the cost of furniture and fixtures. Part of the original Foundation grant was for the support of program during the early years of operation, but as construction costs mounted, the University agreed to underwrite program costs and requested that the amount of the Foundation grant for program be made available for construction. Despite all this, corners had to be cut, and among other things, considerable office space, a service elevator, and air conditioners were eliminated from the original plans in order to save money; later they had to be added at considerably inflated cost.

At Michigan State, however, all costs of building and program were financed through regular university support channels and outside grants from the Foundation and from the Hotel Association of Michigan. At the University of Georgia, special funds were allocated by the governor of the state to make the building of the Center possible. The participation of the Governor of Nebraska, on the other hand, was to serve as chairman of a state-wide fund raising campaign which, through thirty county committees, succeeded in raising more than $1,000,000 in six months through contributions and pledges by more than 5000 individuals and groups from all parts of the state and in all walks of life. Five years later a board member of the Saline County Bank, one of the donors, stated that the board felt its contribution to the Center was probably "the most measurably rewarding and satisfactory contribution the Bank has ever made." A bond issue of $300,000 completed the Nebraska financing.

Although the fund-raising process at each of the first three Kellogg-assisted centers differed, they proceeded without major complications. At Oklahoma and Chicago, however, more scurrying was involved.

The University of Oklahoma had promised to raise $1,300,000 to match the Foundation grant, and, as one university staff member put it, "This proved to be exceedingly difficult."

Despite the governor's support for an appropriation to underwrite the University's share of the Center cost, the legislature appropriated only half, or $650,000. Then, when cost estimates began to come in at $4,250,777, more than double the total initial University obligation plus the Kellogg Foundation's $1,600,000, the University Regents decided to start by constructing only part of the "community in miniature": the Forum, one housing unit, and a dining hall. That would take all but a little more than $24,000 of the money available. (The Foundation agreed but urged complete planning of the total complex so that when money did become available the work could proceed.)

In order to keep things going, the regents authorized the University to issue $1,400,000 worth of self-liquidating dormitory bonds. The bonds were sold at 4.61951%, and then, since the Foundation agreed to advance its total contribution before the bond funds would have to be touched, the entire amount from the bonds were reinvested at a saving of about $50,000 to the University.

The next legislature authorized another $650,000 to complete the original University commitment, but only half was appropriated directly. The rest was to be paid from surpluses which might or might not develop. So, in order to get the Center open on schedule, the University's auxiliary enterprises bought and installed the furnishings, the Center agreeing to reimburse auxiliary enterprises when the second half of the state appropriation came through.

Now funds had been secured for all except an administration building. The University asked Kellogg officials to make the $200,000 originally allocated for program available for the final unit. The Foundation agreed. Then, with some "deletions, adjustments and alterations in site improvements," the University was able to match the $200,000 from Kellogg, and the construction crew proceeded.

Just one part of the original plan—a television studio at the University medical school in Oklahoma City, to facilitate Continuing Education for practicing physicians—had to be abandoned. Otherwise the Oklahoma Center was completed approximately as originally proposed but at almost twice the initial anticipated cost and with payments of some $90,000 a year on the bond issue stretched out ahead.

As a private institution, the University of Chicago had no recourse to governor or legislature. When all normally available funds had been tapped and rising costs still put Center construction out of reach, some severe alterations in the architect's plans had to be made and additional money still had to be borrowed. A hotel consulting firm was retained "to study the newest drawings to determine whether or not the facilities will earn enough to justify the big borrowing." Another worry was whether the architect had reduced the size enough to come within the budget, even with the borrowing.

The Federal Housing and Home Financing Agency did approve a low-interest long-term loan and the building was able to proceed, but with the sacrifice of some essential elements such as well-furnished, well-lighted, conversational alcoves along the halls of the residential area. Payments on the loan, which would have to be met somehow, were to be $110,000 a year.

The University of Notre Dame, another private institution, also had to find funds on its own. Edmund Joyce, University Vice-President, wrote, "The bids were somewhat higher than we had hoped they would be, so that the total cost of the project will be several hundred thousand dollars more than the Kellogg grant. The University will, of course, absorb this additional cost."

One thing appears clear: because the building of a center for Continuing Education is a major project involving educational policy and fiscal responsibility, it is not a task to be undertaken without the philosophical and administrative commitment and support of the institution's central leadership—the governing board and the chief administrative fiscal and academic policy makers—as well as its operating staff and faculty.

## DELAYS CHARACTERISTIC OF CENTER PLANNING

The award of a Foundation grant was cause for celebration, eliciting such responses as "Oh the joy of these days!" from R. W. Tenny, director of short courses at Michigan State when the initial grant was fresh and the first rough plans were being sketched out, and the single word telegram, "Wow!" from Oklahoma's Thurman White in 1958. But characteristic delays diminish enthusiasm. President Hannah said grimly in 1946: "The terrific costs of construction at the moment make it seem probable that if the building is built now we will get only a little more than half as much in the way of a structure as would have been possible prior to the war." When, a year later, the architects Sarvis and Calder completed their working drawings, the cost of the project was estimated at two million dollars and Hannah glumly pointed again to the fact that the cost would be approximately two hundred and twenty percent as much as if they had built in 1939–1940. Yet in 1947 the building was still far from being started and even when the Center opened in 1951, so long had been the delay and so complex had been the administrative and financial problems that many members of the faculty and others dubbed the project "Hannah's Folly."

At the University of Georgia, too, the Foundation grant on November 17, 1953, was followed by a period of delays and frustration. Even though preliminary discussions with architects and other planners had been held prior to the final proposal, it was a month before an arrangement was worked out for a Georgia architectural firm to work in cooperation with the Michigan State architect for the development of the preliminary studies and sketches. From that time until the bids for the beginning of construction were let, three hundred and fifty-eight calendar days were consumed and five hundred more days were needed for the construction. So September 1956—three years from the initial grant—was the date of completion.

However, essential parts of the original proposal had been radio and television stations and a motion picture studio. As the Foundation explained:

"In anticipation of a visit of the Georgia Dairy Association, the Center might broadcast one or several special radio programs or send to the Association a film built around dairy interests. Or, if the audiences were large enough, the television station perhaps would beam a TV program to the group. Then, following the Association's meeting at the Center, radio, TV and film programs would be furnished to the home communities which would summarize and follow through on dairy discussions held at the meeting and thus extend the learning span of members of the group."

The only trouble was that the communications center part of the project presented problems totally different from the relatively simple task of constructing a modern, air conditioned building, even though it involved a hotel-type sleeping wing with comfortably furnished double rooms with bath, with restaurant, snack bar and gift shop, plus a wing for offices, conference rooms of several sizes, and a spectacular hexagonal auditorium patterned after the United Nations General Assembly. Federal Communications Commission regulations with reference to television are complex, and hundreds of hours were involved in what turned out to be relatively unsuccessful negotiations for a suitable transmission tower location for the TV station. In addition, communications equipment was becoming increasingly sophisticated, difficult to obtain, and unexpectedly expensive. Although the technical problems were eventually solved, it was more than ten years after the opening of the facility that a suitable television transmission site—atop famous Stone Mountain—was finally approved. Of all the channels which could be received on the television sets in each of the Center's rooms, the educational channel—the one whose programs were originating in the Center—remained for many years the most difficult to tune in.

DELAYS PLAGUE OTHER CENTERS

Both the Chicago and Oklahoma Centers experienced similar delays between receiving word of the Foundation grant and opening the doors for the public. The Chicago grant was made in 1957 and the Oklahoma grant in 1958. Neither Center was in operation until 1962. In between were periods of exhilaration as verbalized by President Cross of the University of Oklahoma when he accepted the grant, saying that the Foundation's favorable decision "is one of the most gratifying events of my time as president of the University of Oklahoma." But frustration and depression frequently followed. When university officials were thoroughly discouraged over the bleak financial outlook of the future of the proposed center, President Cross announced that it was indefinite when the building could commence. And even when building construction finally did get started, the problems did not cease. As one staff member put it, "The Center presented a sorry picture in the summer and early fall of 1961. So far no site improvements had been made, and the buildings were surrounded by tall weeds and deeply rutted land. The Center lacked sidewalks, hard surface parking, lighting and other needed facilities." Things were so indefinite that on July 5 the *Oklahoma City Times* reported that work had stopped because money had run out. "Until funds are granted," said the paper, "the work will remain halted and the weeds will continue to grow around the buildings."

Although the Nebraska Center was not plagued by the same financial difficulties that caused delays in the building of the other centers, nevertheless bad weather and a labor strike (in which the University was not directly involved) stopped the flow of materials and stilled the sound of hammer, saw, and heavy equipment at a crucial stage in construction.

Oxford University had slightly different problems. As Frank Jessup expressed it:

"An adaptation job of this sort in the early stages involves more destruction than construction, and at the moment the buildings look as though they have been too near high explosive. However, the architect and the builder's foreman seem happy with the way things are going and expect that with the spring and early summer the reconstructed buildings will begin to take recognizable shape."

"The speed at which the work can be done is largely governed by the number of men who can be deployed at any one time, and that number is fairly small because of the awkward building conditions. However, they seem to be going about the work cheerfully, judging from the singing and whistling which permeates Rewley House."

At Durham, New Hampshire, however, the architect's plans for the New England Center so far exceeded the funds available from all means that, although there had occurred the remodeling of a fraternity house to serve as an administration building, bids were not let on the main facility until late in September 1967, even though $1,800,000 had been appropriated by the Foundation in April, 1965. Meanwhile, however, the six New England universities proceeded with the development of pilot programs—presented in various facilities—and continued to search for money for the Center.

## SUCCESS SPELLS TROUBLE AT MICHIGAN STATE

That there probably would be delays along the way between grant and operation was not the only lesson learned in the building of these centers. Another apparent lesson was that, despite the most careful planning, mistakes might be made, and if changes were not effected, the programs might be seriously hampered, a fact that recalls again the words of Winston Churchill.

At Michigan State the initial problem following the opening of the Center was success. Requests for conferences and actual participation were far beyond anyone's most imaginative guess, and by 1953–1954 the building was housing more conferences than it had been designed to accommodate.

The 1951 building had contained one hundred and ninety-three double hotel rooms, dining accommodations for one thousand, an eight-hundred-capacity ballroom, sixteen conference rooms, an auditorium, an elaborate kitchen and administration offices. With the unexpected influx of people, the staff found they needed more conference rooms, particularly large conference rooms, despite the desire to carry on instruction in small classes. The appetite of the adults of the state for Continuing Education was so great that teaching in groups of expanded size was the only alternative to shutting out large numbers of those who wanted to learn. And because of the necessary shifting of equipment to adjust rooms to varying conference needs, the installation of a service elevator—left out originally to save money—became a top priority.

The auditorium had a capacity of only one hundred and fifty people, which was far from adequate, and office space had proved so limited, because of necessary additions to the staff in order to service the influx of conferees, that as many as six people were jammed into a single office.

The Foundation made a grant in November 1954, for additions including two conference rooms, each with the same capacity—one hundred fifty—that had initially been envisioned as an auditorium-sized group. The ballroom was enlarged to provide dining spaces for the largest groups, and was also equipped with folding walls so that parts of it could be used as separate dining rooms for smaller groups of up to one hundred fifty persons each. In addition, twenty feet were added to the front office in order to provide working space for front desk and conference registration personnel.

The architects were able to design the alterations so that the building continued to have the appearance of having been built all at one time. However, the additions were still much too limited. In January 1958, the Foundation agreed to pay half of the cost for still more additions, then estimated at six hundred thousand dollars.

## MATCHING GROUPS TO ROOMS IS COMPLICATED

The basic problem was simply the size and number of the groups. With the original structure and the first alteration, the Center had a total of thirteen conference rooms of various sizes for groups of ten to three hundred and sixty persons.

"However," President Hannah wrote to Dr. Morris, "experience has shown that the five meeting rooms with less than thirty-man capacity can be used for only small breakout groups or planning committee meetings and do not allow for additional conference programs."

Use-analysis of the remaining eight rooms became rather complicated. A survey showed that sixty-five percent of the rooms were in use one hundred percent of the time, the remaining thirty-five percent being in use ninety percent of the time. But increasing the conference capacity thirty-five percent or even ten percent with the existing facilities was simply not possible because handling more conferences required a coincidence in the size of the group requesting the conference and the size of the room still available. Once two-thirds of the available space had been booked, the likelihood that the staff would be able to squeeze new groups into the remaining space was very slight.

"For example," Hannah pointed out, "a recent request for a forty-man, five-day conference 'anytime' between September 15 and December 15, 1957, had to be denied because of lack of meeting room accommodations although sleeping rooms were available during several five-day brackets between those dates."

## THREE-STAGE PLANNING SUGGESTED

The new MSU addition to be financed by the latest Foundation grant was to provide ten additional conference rooms of varying sizes, six to be even more flexible through the installation of folding walls. The auditorium was to be expanded to seat six hundred people. And, as an indication of the tremendous increase in the size of the staff needed to develop and execute the programs which were now serving fifty thousand participants yearly, the addition was also to include thirty new offices. The experience of Michigan State caused the Foundation to suggest that Center development might well be thought of in three stages: original facility; alterations and additions in light of the initial two or three years' experience; final alterations and additions after two or three more years' experience.

At the University of Georgia, too, there were unexpected problems, even though the persons involved in planning and operation had profited from observing the development at Michigan State. In the Georgia Center's first annual report, it was pointed out that one of the big problems was simply handling garbage. There also was the wish that considerably more storage space had been provided and there was a feeling of the need of a separate dining room for banquets or lunches, seating one hundred to one hundred twenty-five persons.

## FLEXIBLE DINING SPACE NEEDED

Actually the original concept had called for a large dining room with an approximate capacity of five hundred people, a cafeteria, snack bar, and small conference dining rooms. However, as construction costs increased, some things obviously had to be changed. The final plans were arrived at through involving as many concerned and informed people as possible—the Center staff, the University faculty and administrative staff, various outside groups over the state, as well as the architects and experienced people from the Foundation. As the result of tight money and the best hunches of advisors, the cafeteria had simply been left out, leaving the large dining room to be supplemented only by one small conference-dining room seating twenty. The thought was that there would be only few occasions when more than three hundred fifty dining spaces would be needed, and the presence in the plant of closed-circuit television was conceived of as permitting overflow banqueteers to meet in conference rooms and observe the program taking place in the large dining room.

Experience proved that solution to be infeasible. In addition, experience showed that there was a great need for several available program-dining spaces simultaneously because a Center the size of Georgia's did not simply accommodate one conference or institute at a time but rather operated a varied and flexible program, sometimes having one large meeting using the building exclusively but more often having three to five smaller institutes operating on parallel or overlapping schedules.

By 1966 Georgia had been able to add a dining wing which provided a banquet room for five hundred, capable of being divided into two to four smaller rooms through the installation of thoroughly soundproof but easily manipulated folding walls. In addition, a snack bar-cafeteria had been developed and proved to be both essential and effective. To serve the increased food needs, Masters had also found it necessary to revamp the kitchen totally, more than doubling its space and completely utilizing new food preparation equipment capable of providing for small as well as large group menus.

Oxford's dining room problem was different. The Secretary wrote:

*"In general, the Center is working admirably. We've met a few problems—the study bedroom over the boiler room, for example, is too warm, even, I suspect, on North American standards, and the dining room reverberates, so we shall have to have the ceiling treated—but these are comparatively small things and can be put right without great expense. The Center has attracted very favourable comment, both within the University, by visitors from other Universities, and above all by participants in conferences in courses held here."*

## EXTENSION OFFICE SPACE ESSENTIAL

At Georgia the clear indication of the need for extensive office space, derived from the Michigan State experience, yielded a plan with sixty-one private and semi-private offices. Another item of tremendous import in twentieth century construction was the realization that the original concept of parking space for three hundred cars was totally inadequate. In the final plan, two parking lots were included, with a total capacity of eight hundred eighty-three cars. This, however, was still not completely adequate, and parking continues to be at a premium. Twenty conference rooms were provided in the Georgia Center. Initial plans called for more than half these to seat twenty-five or fewer persons. Revisions, in the light of discussions before the final plans were approved, reversed the concept and provided for more than half to accommodate thirty or more persons.

## ROUND-TABLES SHOULD NOT BE TOO LARGE

At Oklahoma, where the concept was a complex of buildings reproducing some essential features of a community in miniature, the conference rooms were all built on a hexagonal pattern in order to provide for a round-table discussion setting. There were eighteen small conference rooms each holding twenty-five people, three middle-sized ones for one hundred fifty people, and the large, central Forum with a capacity of five hundred twenty-six. The seats in the main building were built around a central, hydraulically controlled stage which was to provide for varying kinds of equipment and displays to be brought in and out of the auditorium without a great deal of hand-carrying and disturbance. This main building was the focus of admiration on the part of those who visited the opening of the Oklahoma Center. In operation, however, it became apparent that while a round-table discussion was admirable in small groups, the central staging in the large auditorium was most impractical. Faculty members were not used to lecturing from a central pit with their backs to part of the audience all the time. Audio-visual materials were difficult to adapt to the staging situation. As

The larger of the two pictures (*a*) shows the central Forum of the Oklahoma Center, while the smaller (*b*) is of a typical Conference Room A hosting a session in the Forum Building.

a result, the forum had to operate at considerably less than capacity most of the time.

## NOTRE DAME PROFITS FROM OTHERS' EXPERIENCE

When Dean Thomas P. Bergin of Notre Dame was shopping around for ideas to help in the planning of his University's new Center, he noted the necessity for storage of conference room furniture when rooms were being used at less than capacity. Accordingly, he had folding side walls installed so that any equipment not being used could be temporarily placed out of sight, right in the room where it would be needed on a future occasion. This feature eliminated one of the most vexatious physical problems of the conference coordinator—the constant moving of heavy furniture through the halls and from room to room.

Overall, the Notre Dame Center proved to be a most attractive facility. A trade magazine featured it in a January 1967 issue, saying:

*"The large central court, covered by alternate transparent vaulted skylights and roof slabs resting on columns extending above the roof line, provides a feeling of limitless space. The abundance of natural light, the columns separated by small balconies on the second floor, and the porcelain enamel fascia continuing from the exterior right through the court—all combine to create an impression that the court is closely related to the outside environment.*

*"There are ample areas for people to circulate, and lounges for resting or private discussions. Main corridors are designed to serve as convenient display areas.*

*"The central court actually divides the Center in half. A 360-seat auditorium occupies most of one side, extending from the first floor through the mezzanine and second floor. It is equipped with simultaneous translation facilities to accommodate international conferences and multi-language discussion groups.*

*"Some 22 seminar rooms, the essential element of the Center, are spread throughout the building. They vary in size for groups ranging from a half-dozen up to 150 or more. The larger rooms have movable partitions for subdividing. Some of the seminar rooms have equipment to initiate live television programs. All have facilities for tape recording and closed-circuit television.*

*"In the basement of the Center is an audio-visual theatre along with rooms for all types of audio-visual production. It also has a large dining area for special occasions. Normally guests live and dine at the Morris Inn, a University-owned facility connected with the Center by an underground concourse.*

*"It appears that the architects have more than met the challenge of providing the physical and mechanical means for imparting knowledge efficiently, and the aesthetic environment for relaxation between sessions."*

DIRECTORS SHARE ADVICE

Although each Center created a path to adult learning that was appropriate to its own setting, all followed the general route established by the trail-blazing Michigan State Center, profiting from both the insights and oversights of that operation. For example, air conditioning had not been part of the original Michigan State plan, but it rapidly became obvious that when twenty or more people spent six hours in a conference room—even given Michigan's mild summers—heated discussions would be smothered by sheer body heat, and sharp attention would melt into dull lethargy. Georgia and the other Centers were air-conditioned from the start.

Planners visited previously existing Centers and eagerly sought advice from their directors. White of Oklahoma left plans of his proposed "community in miniature" with H. R. Neville, then director of the Continuing Education Center (and now Provost) at Michigan State. Neville wrote back:

*"Without a question you have a very exciting total plan and there are a lot of individual parts within it we would like to have very much, but some questions have occurred to me as I have looked over the plans. In the Forum Building on the second floor, are there permanent desks and permanent chairs installed, and if not, how and where would you store them, if you were to take some of them out to accommodate a different kind of audience?*

*"I don't know whether it would be at all possible to make some kind of an extension on to your dining hall, but you may not be aware of how inefficient it is to get food to the second floor. I don't find any toilet facilities adjacent to the dining hall. I don't know about your people in Oklahoma, but that would never work in Michigan.*

*"I don't see a registration area clearly marked in any of the two housing units or in the Forum Building. As you know, this is one of the problem areas we have had ever since the building opened. We have expanded our conference registration area at least twice and may have to do it again sometime in the future. If I were you, I think I would want to examine Georgia's plan of doing this in a variety of places throughout the buildings before I made my final decision as to how I would handle this very important problem. Our experience shows that registration almost has to be a centrally located office and one which is always in the same place.*

*"Going back to the Forum Building for a minute, where do you plan to store your tables and chairs from the small conference rooms, or do you plan to have them set up permanently with tables and chairs for twenty-five?*

*"In housing unit No. 2, which is the building in which you not only plan to house people but also to have them eat there, I see no office for a building superintendent or conference coordinator. My guess is that before you are in business six months you will be trying to figure out a way to put an office*

*in the building for the person who will be coordinating the various meetings held there. Again, in this building, I see no place for conference or hotel registration.*

*"I guess I have said this before, but I don't see any place in any of your plans or any of your buildings for cloak rooms. Our experience has been that somewhere around one-quarter of our meetings are one-day affairs and I feel relatively sure that yours will be somewhat along the same lines. These people will have some kind of a wrap, especially the women, and you will be looking for a place to hang them before very long.*

*"I notice that you have 300 parking places. I am sure that won't be enough for the 1500 to 2000 people your building will hold. Is there any possibility that you can have an auxiliary parking lot for cars built to the north of this area especially for those who are coming for meals? As you know, it is a long way from your parking lot to the dining hall."*

In answer, Dean White indicated that the desks on the second floor were permanent and that the desks and chairs from the first floor would be stored in the basement; the architects were talking about cloak rooms; the dining hall was going to have toilets in the basement so that "Michiganders will find this building quite comfortable." White indicated that there were going to be mobile registration tables in the Forum Building and other registration areas in the housing units. He also indicated that they were going to have auxiliary parking lots and they were going to put a coat rack or two in each conference room. Later White wrote to the Foundation to say that "the University's housing officials studied and re-studied the kitchen and finally decided it was just too crowded. They cut additional doors to the serving line, installed pass-thru refrigerators from the kitchen to the serving line, put a deep-freeze in the butcher shop, and reduced the bakery to something less than a pie and cake factory.

## KELLOGG CENTERS SHAPE NEW MOVEMENT

But despite extensive planning, consultation and sharing of experience, some of the concepts and constructions still did not function quite as planned. (At Oklahoma the kitchen had to be done over again a year after the Center opened, and further changes were contemplated when more than five years of operation had not killed all the defects.) Nonetheless, the structures which were shaped by visionary adult educators in cooperation with a variety of leading architects, were so successful in their practical innovations that they helped fashion a whole new movement: Continuing Education. The dramatic impact of the multi-storied, multi-purposed specially designed buildings located on the campuses of major educational institutions, strategically selected to cover each section of the United States and to demonstrate the effectiveness of the idea that a building can be part of a teaching team, was immediate and lasting.

In May 1953 the National University Extension Association, one of the most influential of higher education adult education associations, held its annual convention at the Michigan State Kellogg Center. Following the meeting, Edgar L. Harden, at that time director of the Michigan State Center, wrote to Emory Morris of the Kellogg Foundation: "You will be receiving a good many 'orders' for Kellogg Centers as a result of their experiences here." Two weeks later Morris wrote Harden confirming his prediction. "We are being bombarded," Morris said, "more and more for information and advice concerning your activities." By the end of July, Harden had spent a week in California at the invitation of the chancellors, deans and regents at Santa Barbara and the University of California campus at Berkeley. He had also talked with the presidents at the Universities of Nebraska and Rhode Island about the building and operation of a center. The University of Colorado had been in contact with him by telegraph. "It all goes to show," Harden told Morris, "that we might have under way the

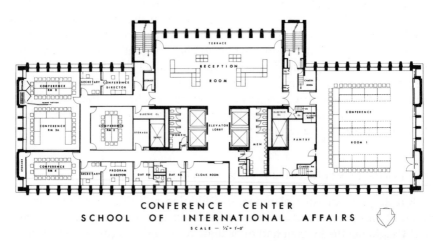

CONFERENCE    CENTER
SCHOOL    OF    INTERNATIONAL    AFFAIRS
SCALE — ¼" = 1'-0"

Shown is the heart of the Columbia University Conference Center which will occupy the whole of the fifteenth floor of the School of International Affairs Building. There are five well-arranged conference rooms, offices, a large reception room, a pantry to facilitate use of the area for receptions, luncheons, and dinners, as well as camera and interpreters booths for the main conference room. A control room for live and closed circuit television is in the lower part of the building. Each of the tower floors below the conference floor will have a conference room, and an auditorium on the ground floor will be available for conference use.

most important development in American Education since the establishment of the public school system."

And what was this innovation? Most visibly it was a building, a large one, modern in every respect and equipped throughout with carpeting, furniture and conveniences of the latest and best design and construction available. It was a building to be used by adults, and so everything in the building was conceived on an adult scale. But it was also a building to be used for education, so everything in it was oriented toward making learning attractive and effective for the adult students who would participate. The facility was located on the campus of a major university in order that the participants—faculty and students—could take advantage of the total educational resources of the institution. The building was designed to provide all the needs of the students and faculty during the conduct of a course: housing, feeding, teaching, and relaxing. But, above all, the building was just one part of the superstructure; to both planners and operating staff it was always clear: program is the base and learning is the goal.

CHAPTER 4

# Continuing Education in Action: Program Planning and Presentation

The government officials who flew into Chicago for a national conference on air pollution prevention, the dentists studying at Lincoln the latest developments in roentgenology, the Nebraska farm youths discussing agricultural prospects, and the scientists involved in space-age technology at the University of Oklahoma, all were demonstrating residential Continuing Education in action. So was the young man trying to become a better resort operator in Michigan, the Negro farmer, and the newly elected state legislator meeting with colleagues in Georgia, the theologians exploring ecumenicism at Notre Dame, and the adult educators from several nations exchanging views at Rewley House, Oxford, England. The meetings in which they were involved all came about as the result of similar patterns of program planning and proceeded through similar stages of participant involvement, despite vast differences in program content and structure.

The first push can come from practically any direction. However, three principal sources for program ideas and conference initiation are: (a) members of the Center staff; (b) members of the faculty, and (c) members of community or business and professional organizations.

With regard to Center staff members as initiators of conferences, the Assistant Dean for business and industrial services at the Oklahoma Center, points out that his staff "serves as liaison between the University and the practicing professional; we see our job as awareness of the resources of the University staff and the needs of the professional; and we try to bring these two together." In Oklahoma (a petroleum-producing area) for example, one member of the staff believed that intensive work in advanced geology was needed. He expressed his idea to several faculty members and professionals and found that they agreed. As a result, he called together a committee of faculty geologists and practitioners from business and industry who worked with him to narrow the topic to teachable specifics, to select a teaching staff, and to suggest individuals and organizations who might participate as sponsors and students. "Apparently," said the Assistant Dean, "the advice we received about this was good because the course has been oversubscribed right from the start."

Faculty members are also the source for many program ideas. At the University of Nebraska, the chairman of the Department of Veterinary Science and an associate professor of Animal Science were having coffee together during a break between summer classes and discovered that both were receiving an unusual number of calls from large stock producers about lame hogs. Later, they approached the Director of the Department of Conferences and Institutes at the Nebraska Center.

"We want to put on a short course for some of Nebraska's large commercial swine producers," the animal scientist said. "We've lined up a number of people from our own faculties and some off-campus people. What do you think the possibilities are?"

The staff worked with the two faculty members and with representatives of the Swine Producers' Association, developing a two-day program. Among the contributions of the Nebraska Center staff were suggestions for course design, including a combination of introductory lectures supplemented by audio-visual materials, provision for a laboratory field trip to observe on-the-farm examination and remedial action, and follow-up, small discussion sessions to apply the knowledge gained to specific situations. Several meetings and a great deal of detailed planning preceded the successful seminars, but the team of faculty, Center staff, and outside organizations was able to take the professors' ideas and implement them effectively, not only through course design but also through the development of specially prepared pre- and post-conference reference materials.

More than one-fourth of the programs at Centers for Continuing Education are developed to meet a need identified by groups outside the University. A committee representing the personnel managers of several governmental departments in the Michigan State Capitol met with Dr. Armand Hunter, Director of the Continuing Education Service at Michigan State University.

"Communications," they said, "is our most serious problem."

"Communications is a catch-all kind of word," Hunter pointed out. "We need to identify the kinds of problems you want to solve. Then maybe we can talk about the kinds of people and the shape of program that would help you to do the job." He reached for his telephone. "Let me get our director of conferences in on this," he said, "and he and his staff will help you determine your objectives and the best ways of achieving them."

"I guess what we mean is that people don't seem to want to help each other," the personnel chief said when Dr. Tunis Dekker, the conference director, had joined them. "There are invisible walls between departments and between people at desks right next to each other. It's as if each person was trying to keep what he was doing secret from everybody else."

"It isn't that they're fighting each other or anything," one of the other personnel men said, "it's just that they're not helping, not talking things over, not working things out together."

"You want to set up a program that will help change the thinking, the feelings and the actions of the whole state personnel group, don't you?" Dekker asked.

"I guess that's just about it," the personnel chief agreed.

"Well, let's get at it, then," Dekker said.

Within his staff, Dekker assigned a conference coordinator to work with the personnel group and to initiate what he has termed the "conference cycle," in which the conference coordinator, as an "educator-administrator," guides the planning group in:

1. Determining what characteristics of the student group will influence educational considerations of the program;

2. Setting up educational objectives and desired outcomes for the conference;

3. Selecting the content and learning experiences to accomplish the objectives and achieve the desired outcomes;

4. Choosing instructors and leaders and organizing learning experiences for effective instruction;

5. Arranging for finances;

6. Selecting and making arrangement for physical facilities and services;

7. Disseminating information which will reach the public or publics that have an interest in accomplishing the objectives as set forth by the planners;

8. Coordinating and shepherding the conference during presentation;

9. Developing plans for conference evaluation and a follow-up study to determine whether any behavior changes have taken place as a consequence of the conference.

## TEAM CONCEPT ESSENTIAL

The essential ingredient for successful residential Continuing Education as developed at the Kellogg-assisted centers is the conference and institute team. The team concept involves not only the joint planning by community groups, university faculty and continuing education staffs, but also by an internal team in the center itself. This team shares the responsibility for program planning and presentation, participant recruitment and accommodation, and financial and technical program support.

Typical of routine practice at the several centers was the Community Development Conference held at the Nebraska Center in the fall of 1965. It started the summer before when the president of the Nebraska Junior Chamber of Commerce was visiting with board members of a Jaycee chapter in the western part of the state.

"You know," the Jaycee president said, "the way you guys were able to get community support for that new swimming pool is pretty impressive. I think it would help a lot of the other chapters to get things done if we could figure out some way for you to tell them the story of how you got this project shaped up."

"The Nebraska Center has a way," one of the local Jaycees said. "I've attended seminars there on civic affairs and management development and they really know how to set up a program."

So the Jaycee president and his education chairman arranged to visit the campus for a conversation with Dean Edward Janike of the Extension Division.

"Jaycees are dedicated to civic improvement," the Jaycee president explained, "but we're neophytes in the business of organizing and carrying out programs. Our communities all contributed to the building of this Nebraska Center and now we're asking your help in designing and presenting a conference for the practical discussion of ways and means to make our Nebraska communities better places to live in."

"Good," Dean Janike said, "that's what we've been for. The first step is to talk with Art Ward, head of conferences and institutes."

"It sounds to me like the kind of thing we have in mind is right down Otto Hoiberg's alley," Dr. Ward said, after the project was explained to him. "Otto's director of our Department of Community Development and is a real authority in the field. I'll call him and see if he can sit in on the rest of the session with us."

Hoiberg joined the group and agreed to assist in planning the conference and to participate as a discussion leader once the session started. The group consulted the master calendar in Dr. Ward's office and decided that the weekend of November 10 and 11 would be a good time for the conference; space would be available in the Center, and the Jaycee representatives felt that members would find it possible to come to the campus for a weekend meeting at that time of the year more easily than either mid-week or a later period that might run into the Christmas holiday business rush. The meeting adjourned with the Jaycees agreeing to seek out three or four people from their group to make presentations on successful community projects and with Hoiberg agreeing to give a talk on general community development principles. A sub-committee was formed to work with the coordinator in developing a plan and in selecting faculty leaders for group discussions of practical problems and methods for solving them.

## CONFERENCE COORDINATOR IS KEY MAN

Following the initial planning sessions, the conference coordinator immediately began to grapple with the paperwork designed to keep details straight and all members of the team informed. First there was the University "conference request form." This got down on paper such information as the following:

1. The person originating the request for the conference and the date of the request. (The Jaycee president.)

2. A suggested conference title. (Community Improvement Seminar.)

3. An indication of whether a similar conference had previously been held at the University of Nebraska or whether this was a new one. (New.)

4. A statement of the purpose and objectives of the conference. (To establish principles and projects for community improvement.)

5. The department or college expected to serve as University sponsor. (Community Development.)

6. The kinds of people expected to attend, anticipated attendance and groups to be served. (100 Jaycees.)

7. Identification of individuals and groups involved in planning. (Jaycees, Center, Community Development Department.)

8. Conference dates.

Next he sent through a University "conference endorsement form" so that Hoiberg's department and college would officially signify its sponsorship of the event.

In order to be sure that appropriate rooms would be reserved and the conference would be taken into consideration in food plans, the coordinator made out a "conference rooms and food reservation form" indicating how many overnight rooms would probably be needed, what dining rooms he wanted for luncheons or dinners, and what conference rooms should be set aside for the institute.

## COORDINATOR WORKS WITH COMMITTEE

Working with the department and the Jaycee committee, the coordinator was able to predict an attendance of about one hundred with perhaps half wanting single rooms and half being willing to share a twin bedroom with a friend. The planners decided on a group luncheon each day and a group dinner Saturday evening. They would need the auditorium for their general sessions all Saturday morning and the first hour in the afternoon, as well as for a final session Sunday afternoon. In addition, they would need five small conference rooms for discussions Saturday afternoon and Sunday morning.

As program plans developed, the coordinator sent through requests for faculty participation to various departments, both to get suggestions from department chairmen and college deans and to insure in writing that everybody concerned knew who would be involved, when, where and why. The form also provided a space for the department chairman and dean to indicate whether they believed that faculty service should be provided without charge, whether the conference should be charged for the service and a transfer made to a departmental budget, or whether the individual faculty member should be paid directly for his participation. The coordinator reported results of his queries to the planning committee by mail, and followed through on confirming speaker selection as decided at their meetings.

As the coordinator moved toward getting a printed brochure out to prospective conference participants, he sent a request for a biographical sketch to each of the prospective discussion leaders or speakers. He also sent along a "speaker's audio-visual form," giving each faculty or non-faculty member a chance to indicate in advance what kind of audio-visual equipment he would need, so that the coordinator, in turn, could make reservations for equipment with the Bureau of Audio-Visual Instruction of the University's Extension Division.

When the copy for the brochure was complete, the coordinator filled out a "printing and mailing request," indicating exactly how many copies of the brochure would be printed, to whom they would be mailed, the class of mail, and the methods of distribution.

By this time the actual conference dates were approaching and the coordinator had to come to grips with specific room arrangements in order to make out a "room set-up request" for the housekeeping staff. In the auditorium he needed a speaker's table for a chairman and two participants. For the discussion groups, he chose an O-shaped table arrangement, with chairs around the outside.

A similar kind of information needed to be sent to the conference food service indicating the date, time, place and number of people who would be sharing the planned luncheons and suppers. The specific numbers of meals to be served for each group had to be guaranteed twenty-four hours in advance, a fact which gave everyone jitters, since from none of the groups were the reservations totally received, even that close to conference time.

## THE PROGRAM BEGINS

Subsequent face-to-face meetings between the members of the original planning committee, augmented by additional Jaycees, several long distance telephone conversations, chats with faculty participants, and voluminous mail, preceeded the arrival on the evening of Friday, December 9, of the first conference participant. The coordinator stood at one side of the room registration desk as a young Jaycee from Wahoo set his suitcase on the floor and filled in the room slip. After that, the Jaycees began to come in through the lobby's three sets of doors in increasing numbers.

Many of the participants knew each other from other meetings in other places, and the conversation level next morning was high as they strolled into the auditorium from their individually ordered breakfasts in the Hall of Youth cafeteria; but the talk was about back home, business, and a book or two—not about the subject of the session, community development.

Dean Janike welcomed the Jaycees to the Nebraska Center and turned the day over to the Jaycees' own program chairman, who introduced the president of the Lincoln Chamber of Commerce as opening speaker. Then

A conferring group at the Nebraska Center is intent upon a problem.

a member of the Junior Chamber of Commerce chapter from Ogalala told about how his group had decided the old, wooden, weathered railroad station in their town was an eyesore and something had better be done about it. He told of conferences with businessmen, with the mayor and council, with railroad representatives and others, going step by step through the process from conceiving the idea that the old station had to go, to the dedication ceremony for the new modern depot that had replaced it. Before he finished his talk, the coordinator had slipped out of the auditorium to make sure that the coffee urn, rolls and cups were in place in the second floor lobby for a coffee break which followed the Ogalala talk.

## FOOD SERVICE POSES PROBLEMS

Conversation was somewhat more directed to community development from the auditorium to the coffee line, and it continued until the second case study, the building of a new school house at Beatrice, was presented. The coordinator didn't hear that talk or the one that followed because, despite all his planning, a crisis had come up with the food service: twelve Jaycees had come in late without advance registrations and they wanted to get in on the group luncheon. Unfortunately, there was room for only six extra settings and the coordinator decided it would be best not to split the late group so he slipped back into the auditorium to announce from the stage, before the group broke up for lunch, that only those who had made advance registrations for luncheons could be seated in the Columbus room and the others would have to go to the restaurant and miss the luncheon program.

After lunch there was one more session in the auditorium at which were utilized slides, charts and a short motion picture to illustrate the principles of community development involved in seeking out the power structure and mobilizing public opinion for civic improvement. Then the group broke up into five regional discussion sessions, and the coordinator, moving from room to room, observed how one or two participants seemed to dominate each group at the outset but how, with guidance and control by the faculty leaders, the discussions soon became specific, enthusiastic, and focused on identifying jobs to be done and ways to do them based on the concepts that Professor Hoiberg had presented.

## DISCUSSION CONTINUES INTO NIGHT

Some of the group went out on the town after the evening banquet at which a number of the business faculty related community development to good business, but many formed shifting groups in both the first and second floor lobbies to carry on the discussion of the afternoon and argue about the points raised by the banquet speaker. The coordinator knew, too, that additional conversations were going on in the rooms that comprised the sleeping wing of the Nebraska Center.

Next morning, though, the discussions got off to a slow start, as if everyone had talked himself out the night before. But skilled prodding by the discussion leaders provoked attention to the desirability of focussing in on the selection of projects to work on back home, and everyone began to get very verbal and involved as the hands of the clock told them it was close to lunch time and the end of their discussion sessions.

A luncheon speaker from the College of Agriculture talked about trends in farming that would affect the rural community, and the final general session gave a representative of each discussion group a chance to report back to the total conference.

As the participants checked out, talk was about the things they were going to accomplish and what they would have to report when they met in the Nebraska Center next year.

## CONFERENCES FOLLOW A PATTERN

What had happened to the Jaycees' Community Development conference was typical in the planning and presentation of hundreds of seminars on a vast number of subjects, involving a wide variety of group sponsors in other Continuing Education Centers across the country. The pattern of these conferences had been predicted by Professor Houle at the University of Chicago several years earlier when he outlined the course of an adult conference as:

1. A period of orientation.
2. A settling down to work.
3. A midway slump.
4. A period of unusually heavy activity and the desire to get everything accomplished.
5. A final period of culmination characterized by high morale.

Another important factor is the conference director, himself. Studies have shown that he is a key figure who influences at least some of the general shaping of the program. In order to understand the conceptions, skills, knowledge and values of this key figure, Dr. Donald A. Deppe, Director of Conferences and Institutes at the University of Maryland, interviewed forty-five other conference directors in forty-one United States universities and was able to identify five basic orientations which influenced the design and development of conferences under these directors' leadership.

The "client-oriented" conference director, Deppe found, considered himself "in a people business," and concentrated his generative activity on "identifying faculty persons who are especially skilled in dealing with adult students, and involving such 'rare staff members' in programs of continuing education." This type of conference director, according to Deppe, believes that the people must be served and he is there to see that they are served well.

The "operations-oriented" conference director is concerned about the smooth running of the program and is particularly eager to develop conferences that provide challenging and intricate details to be coordinated, such as simultaneous translations, complicated audio-visual aids, or television broadcasting. His chief satisfaction, according to Deppe, consists in the knowledge of a job well done.

The "image-oriented" conference director feels that "he *is* the university" to the groups with which he deals, and is concerned that his programs project a favorable image of the university. He tends to generate programs that will involve key publics of the university such as parents and legislators, and he is particularly gratified to hear people speak well of the university as a result of attendance at a conference in his center.

The "institution-oriented" conference director is imaginatively generative within the university but is cautious in responding to external requests. He believes that high-level programming is shaped and projected by the university and not by those outside. "To him the traditions of scholarship within the university are sacred, and he is there to see that they are not sacrificed."

Finally, the "problem-oriented" conference director "sees problems in society that cry out for solution," and he tries to mobilize the educational resources available to him in order to try to solve those problems. He frequently succeeds in "bending time-honored traditions" and feels that "both the university and society benefit in this process." Eight of the forty-five conference directors in the study appeared to be problem-oriented, and Deppe suggested that they might represent "a new and highly sophisticated type of leadership within the field."

But whatever the leadership orientation, the planning and presentation process is similar at all residential conference centers. There is the planning committee made up of faculty, community, and staff coordinator; there is the planning process, focusing on identification of objectives, selection of topics, involvement of the rich resources of the universities in which the centers are located, and the shaping of conference design, usually consisting of a combination of lectures, panels or symposiums, discussion or work groups, and independent study or work projects. There is the facilitation procedure concerned with selection of dates, arrangements for rooms, meals,

A Conference on the Humanities at Notre Dame.

Conference directors in the Foundation-aided Centers are concerned about the smooth-running of program and give particular attention to the coordination of auxiliary details including simultaneous translations, complicated audio-visual arrangements, and telecasting. Pictures *a* to *g* present glimpses of conferences varying in size, in facilities, and in types of participants.

Gas Compressor Short Course in session in Conference Room "B" in the Forum Building at the University of Oklahoma's Center for Continuing Education.

72

Executive Management Seminar at Michigan State University.

The distaff side at the University of Oxford.

73

A "For Women Only" Conference at Michigan State University.

Audio-visual needs and instructional aids of any conference can be readily met by the University of Chicago's Center for Continuing Education which maintains its own staff for these services.

74

(g)

Conference rooms at the University of Chicago's Center for Continuing Education vary from intimate lounges, such as seen here, which can accommodate up to 40 or 50 people theater style, through expandable conference rooms which can seat 150 persons, with an assembly seating 300. All conference rooms are air-conditioned, can be physically set-up to suit the format of almost any meeting.

audio-visual aids and reference material, brochure printing and distribution, publicity, advance registrations, room set-ups, and reception, identification or orientation of participants; there is, finally, the presentation phase which necessitates the checking and supervision of all plans and the creative adjustment to change.

Although that is the general trace, the presence of the flexible and innovative planning and presentation team, the dynamic resource of university faculties and facilities, and the sheer existence of a specially designed structure—tacitly demanding to be used, explored and stretched from wall to wall, foundation to roof, and microphone to microwave—stimulates creative programming, bringing new worlds of knowledge through new methods and media to new generations of adult learners.

## CHICAGO RECEIVES CREATIVITY AWARDS

At the University of Chicago, Dr. Sol Tax, Dean of Extension, has carefully explicated patterns of presentation that have resulted in creativity awards from the National University Extension Association. He said:

*"In the last two academic years, the Center for Continuing Education has established two major conference models and has experimented with others. These models were intended to test two propositions: one, that a carefully designed conference could contribute significantly to the understanding and the ultimate solution of important issues of public policies; two, that an appropriately structured conference could accelerate the advancement of scientific knowledge in a given area by integrating the existing research in that area, by generating new research through a confrontation of relevant scholars and sciences, and by diffusing new knowledge to a wider group of specialists. Recently conferences at the Center for Continuing Education have established the validity of both propositions, and indeed have produced results which have far surpassed expectations. The two models have been, respectively, public affairs conferences and frontiers of knowledge conferences."*

One of the public affairs conferences, to which Dr. Tax referred, was the "Conference on the Draft" held December 4 to 7, 1966. The University assembled approximately 125 scholars, educators, military specialists, students and young people, as well as members of the Congress and leaders of national civic, religious and special interest groups. Papers were written especially for the conference and were circulated well in advance, eliminating long, formal presentations so that three full days could thus be devoted to an examination of advantages and disadvantages of the present system and the consideration of major alternatives. The conference received extensive coverage in all news media. Congressmen in attendance at the conference reported their intention of carrying the result of the conference to the forthcoming congressional debate. Papers prepared for the conference and conference proceedings were to be published in a book in the spring of 1967.

Another public affairs conference was the "China Conference" held in February 1966 which, according to Tax, "probably influenced the subsequent Fulbright committee hearings in the U.S. Senate." A group of international experts brought together the facts on mainland China and suggested interpretations of the facts and pointed out possible consequences of various policies.

Both conferences shared a basic approach which is reflected in the carefully planned procedure: first, a faculty planning committee of substantive experts from various disciplines was assembled and the staff coordinators

Conferences on any subject and participated in by any group are carefully structured at Continuing Education Centers. Staff and faculty planning are first steps, followed by communications with and planning by the sponsoring organizations. Shown is a staff planning session at the Chicago Center for Continuing Education, with Mrs. Lucy Ann Marx, Center Director, in the background.

assigned. Outside organizations were brought in when appropriate. A group of about forty to fifty panelists was then invited to participate in the conference and to prepare the papers in advance. Papers were reproduced and distributed well before the conference thus permitting the entire conference to be devoted to substantive discussion. A second group, composed of other experts and representatives of interested organizations, also received advance papers and prepared to enter into the conference deliberations. A third group of key representatives of the press was also invited. As Tax described the meeting:

*"All sessions of the conference are plenary. The conference chamber is arranged in three concentric squares, panelists in the inner square and other participants and press in the outer squares. The inner square is equipped with forty microphones controlled by an operator at the computerized console. Thus, perfect sound is assured and broadcast quality tape recordings of the entire conference are made. Public affairs conferences culminate in one or more public sessions for large audiences, receive wide public exposure through the press, radio, television, and are designed to be followed by quick publication of conference papers and procedures."*

The "Conference on the Origins of Man" was the first fully developed "frontiers of knowledge" conference held in the Chicago Center for Continuing Education. Some one hundred fifty participants, including thirty distinguished scientists from both the United States and abroad, took part in the three-day symposium in April 1965, at which Lewis S. B. Leakey, Director of the Corynden Memorial Museum in Nairobi, Kenya, released new evidence of early man based upon his findings of fossil remains in lower strata of deposits in Olduvai Gorge. Of the meeting, Tax said, "This conference provided a unique opportunity for the presentation of important new findings to an assemblage of scholars who, in turn, had the opportunity to evaluate the findings and discuss directions for further research." An audience of over one hundred teachers and students of anthropology attended the conference which provided them an opportunity to become acquainted with the latest research in the field. Finally, results of the conference were widely disseminated through press, radio, and television coverage and, ultimately, by publication of the proceedings. This conference was followed a year later by a similar three-day seminar on "Man the Hunter" with a third conference of this type, "Peasant and Village Culture," in 1967.

## NEW ENGLAND DEVELOPS REGIONAL PROGRAMS

In New Hampshire, where, in 1967, a fraternity house was being remodeled to serve as an administration building, and ground had not yet been broken for the first residential unit of the New England Center, the six states in the combined enterprise utilized the facilities of the nearby Exeter House, guest inn for Phillips Exeter Academy, as the site for several pre-center projects. One week-long residential session brought together commissioners of administration and other principal officers from the six states. That such meetings were both rare and needed was demonstrated when New Hampshire's President, John McConnell, and Dr. Arthur Adams found themselves introducing counterparts in adjacent state administrations, and even members of the same state administration, to each other since never before had they come together to discuss their mutual problems.

Another week-long pilot project at the New England Center was a ten-day conference sponsored by the Adult Education Association of the U.S.A. (A.E.A.) and financed by a grant from the Administration on Aging of the U.S. Department of Health, Education and Welfare. The session, entitled "Enriching the Later Years Through Learning," brought together representatives of thirty organizations of six New England States—schools, libraries, universities, government organizations, churches, community centers and others—to meet with fifteen A.E.A. staff members from all over the United States to discuss ways and means of making retirement a time to learn, and to study many of the interesting things in life that could contribute to good living in the later years.

But perhaps the most relevant to continuing education of the pre-center conferences was one held at the W. Alton Jones Campus of the University of Rhode Island. It brought together representatives of both Cooperative (Agricultural) Extension and General Extension of the six state universities to move "Toward Meeting the Needs of Continuing Education in New England."

Financed with funds provided through a Kellogg Foundation programming grant, the idea grew out of informal discussions during June 1966, leading to a decision by the Center director in August to appoint a formal planning committee of representatives from the six universities plus the New England Center staff and the staff of Boston University's Center for the Study of Liberal Education for Adults. The committee met in September, and the conference was held October 25 to 27, when the state university presidents were to be on hand for a meeting with the New England Board of Higher Education.

As background material, each representative provided a summary of the Continuing Education activities on his campus. Dr. Harry Day, New England Center director, said of the affair:

*"From the outset, a note of informality permeated the proceedings. Considering the fact that the cooperative and general extension people had never been brought together before, there was a refreshing degree of candor. Certainly*

The rising New England Center facility has a Thoreau-like, wooded retreat site which is expected to add much to the learning atmosphere.

*the New England Center site, itself, a beautiful, wooded retreat, added much to the general atmosphere."*

National issues were delineated by Dr. Paul A. Miller, Assistant Secretary of Health, Education and Welfare, and his remarks were later published in an *Occasional Paper,* a device the New England Center proposed to use frequently to disseminate cogent parts of conference programs.

State and local issues were reviewed by Dr. A. A. Liveright, Director of CSLEA, who had analyzed the summaries of state university programs. President Francis H. Horn of the University of Rhode Island presented the views of a university chief administrator.

Summing up, Dr. Day said:

*"Judging by the many favorable responses of the participants, the conference accomplished considerable headway on two counts: (a) the cooperative and general extension people of the region were able to share ideas in an atmosphere conducive to a full examination of mutual interests; (b) the participants were unanimous in their support of a set of recommendations growing out of small group discussion regarding the possible next steps for continuing education in the six state region."*

## COLUMBIA HAS LEADERSHIP CONFERENCE

As the construction of its International Affairs Conference Center proceeded, Columbia University, like the New England group, initiated exploratory conferences at other sites. One such session was a "Conference on Leadership," sponsored jointly by Columbia's Institute on War and Peace Studies and *Daedalus,* the Journal of the American Academy of Arts and Sciences. Held at Sterling Forest, Tuxedo, New York, the conference assembled twenty-two American social science scholars to consider for three days such topics as "The Identity Crisis and Weak Presidents," "The Theory of Charismatic Leadership," "Political Leadership and Social Change in American Cities," "Obstacles to the Perception of Change in Under-Developed Countries," and "The Power of Intellect and the Politics of Ideas."

Full drafts or detailed outlines of articles on the discussion topics were circulated to participants in advance. The discussion at the conference concentrated on exploring a number of convergent approaches to the study of leadership. Of the conference, Dean Andrew Cordier said:

"Informal comments at the conference itself and subsequent reactions seem to indicate that the participants without exception considered this meeting one of the most fruitful and rewarding conferences among the many

Pictured are some of the consultants for a "Conference on Leadership" sponsored jointly by Columbia's Institute on War and Peace Studies and *Daedalus,* the Journal of the American Academy of Arts and Sciences. With the Columbia International Affairs Conference Center under construction, the meeting was held at Sterling Forest, Tuxedo, New York.

that each of them had attended. The authors of reports started from the perspective of different disciplines, such as political science and history. The leadership situations they investigated ranged in time from the early eighteenth century to the present, in space over five continents. Some of the leaders examined were founders of states or of nationalist movements; others were the originators of major intellectual trends in natural or social science. A third group of papers dealt with the setting of the process of leadership in situations as diverse as crises of food supply in primitive societies, the formulation of policies for economic development in contemporary Latin America, and the need for urban reform in the United States today. Nonetheless, a common set of questions about the psychological, intellectual, and political aspects of leadership clearly seemed to emerge from the three days of discussion."

Follow-up plans included an issue of *Daedalus* containing the papers in final, revised form, publication in hard covers by Houghton-Mifflin, and in paperback by the Beacon Press so that wide distribution could be made, not only to scholars but also to the concerned general public.

## GEORGIA DEVELOPS "DOCU-DRAMA"

At the University of Georgia, where "communications" had been an essential of the original Center plans, a vital new form of presentation called "Docu-drama" was developed for use within the Center and throughout the state to present provocative material on critical issues through the use of light, color, sound, words, pictures, and action. One docu-drama, "Don't Let This Happen to Johnny," was developed by the program staff headed by Dr. T. W. Mahler, through the Center's communication facilities, involving the motion picture production staff, the art department, printing department, subject matter coordinator, writers, and actors.

This work was done in response to a request from a joint committee of the Georgia Federation of Women's Clubs and the United Church Women of Georgia who had a project under way focused on getting Georgia children out of common jails. The docu-drama was presented first at the Georgia Center for a statewide conference of women's clubs representatives and church women. The script, slides, film clips, and tapes necessary for presentation of the docu-drama were then made available to the clubs so that it could be presented in the local communities of the state. In addition, a discussion guide was prepared to be used following each presentation of the docu-drama to various community groups in church halls, civic auditoriums, and the like. The effort in a docu-drama is to shock, involve and thereby inform the viewer.

Some excerpts from "Don't Let This Happen to Johnny" illustrate the method:

LIGHT CUE.   *Shadow screen light fades up and spot No. 3 out.*
SOUND CUE.   *Roll tape No.2.*

   (*Boy, Johnny is sitting in the chair behind the shadow screen*)
TAPE.

     JUDGE.   Has the jury reached a verdict?
     JUROR.   We have, your honor.
     JUDGE.   The defendent will rise for the verdict.
     (*Johnny rises from the chair*)
     JUDGE.   What is your verdict?
     JUROR.   We find the defendant guilty of armed robbery.
     JUDGE.   You have heard the verdict of your peers. I sentence you
              to two years in prison. (*Johnny slumps into his chair*) Court
              will adjourn until tomorrow at nine.
    *Sound of people talking as they leave court.*

SHOW SLIDE NO. 1.   *Newspaper with headline U.S. Reaching New Heights.*
SOUND CUE.   *Roll tape No. 3.*

TAPE.

NEWSBOY.    Extra, extra! Read all about it. Read all about the U.S. space program. Scientist say U.S. can hit moon.

*Traffic sounds under and out by end of next speech.*

SHOW SLIDE NO. 2.    *Girl hiding face.*

ONE.    Juvenile delinquency sky-rockets. Atlanta, Georgia: In the past four years, juvenile offenders appearing in Fulton County Courts increased 110%.

TWO.    In recent report on juvenile delinquency, H. W. Hurt says, "Character is caught, not taught."

ONE.    U.S. scientists worry over diminishing natural resources.

TWO.    Sheriff Joseph D. Lohman says, "America's number one resource is its young people."

THREE.    The National Probation and Parole Association reports: Every year, across the country, fully 100,000 boys and girls from seven to seventeen are held in county jails and police lockups, most of them substandard even for adults. Thousands more youngsters are held in basement cells or behind bars in so-called detention homes—medieval monstrosities which, in effect, are children's dungeons.

SHOW SLIDE NO. 3.    *Justice versus geography.*

ONE.    Justice is a matter of geography in Georgia; Sixteen year old juvenile delinquent sentenced to twenty years in prison for theft of thirty dollars.

TWO.    Mrs. Margaret Burton of DeKalb County, doctor-fleecing fame, got out today after serving 18 months, her debt for embezzling $186,000 completed.

SHOW SLIDE NO. 4.    *Hypo needle and bottles.*

ONE.    Drugs found in possession of prisoners at Reidsville.

SHOW SLIDE NO. 5.    *Face of screaming boy.*

ONE.    Crowded conditions cause riots.

TWO.    The King County Jail in another state contains 400 prisoners with one warden to care for them. Seven of these prisoners are teenagers placed together in a bull pen. The warden later explained, "When you have to put seven boys in one room, there's bound to be a lot of rough housing. They will scream until we have to threaten to put them in cells we don't have." Later this evening one of the boys beat another to death with a shower handle.

LIGHT CUE.    *Spot No. 3 on. Slide projector off.*

LIVE.

REPORTER.    "These things are going on today. It's the way things are."

LIGHT CUE.    *Spot No. 1 on.*

JUDGE.    Excuse me, but I feel I should be allowed a word in defense of the judges and courts of Georgia, as well as in other states. We don't want to put children in inadequate detention homes. We don't want to return children to society not yet rehabilitated, but we do. We do because it's all we have power to do.

In his discussion guide, Mahler says:

"The docu-drama, if effectively presented, will disturb the viewer emotionally. Each viewer in all probability will attempt to restore his equilibrium by following one of two approaches. Some will immediately concern themselves with things that ought to be done to improve the present situation in Georgia. Others will attempt to rationalize and explain away the current situation by attempting to convince themselves and others that the docu-drama is exaggerated and that things are not as bad as presented. It is the purpose of the follow-up discussion to capitalize on this concern by discussing some of the questions involved in the handling of delinquents as well as adult offenders. The discussion leaders should attempt to avoid useless arguments as to whether or not the docu-drama is over-exaggerated by stating that it is designed to create concern and was put in docu-drama form for this purpose. Even so, the material has been checked with subject-matter experts and with practicing juvenile court judges who state that they have encountered many actual cases, even more extreme than the composite one developed in the docu-drama."

With regard to the docu-drama, "Don't Let This Happen to Johnny," it was noted that the two women's organizations, "on their own," created a tremendous amount of interest in penal reform and in revitalizing the work of the State Department of Welfare. During the gubernatorial campaign of that year the successful candidate, Carl Sanders, endorsed penal reform with particular emphasis on the juvenile offender and expansion and improvement in the state welfare program. After installation in office, Governor Sanders increased appropriations to these departments. He also took the leadership in initiating enabling legislation for expanding and enriching the programs of these two departments and helped them secure additional staff and more competent leadership personnel. The Center's role was primarily that of helping the citizens at the grass-root level focus on the problem of the treatment of the juvenile criminal offender through use of the docu-drama and subsequent discussion sessions. It took no part in the political activity of the two women's groups who were seeking the reforms.

The docu-drama not only illustrates the creative development of a striking educational technique but also suggests—as did the New Hampshire programs—what might be termed the "outreach" phase of Continuing Education involving program presentation outside the Center as well as in the facility itself.

## OKLAHOMA B.L.S. DEGREE IS NEW

At the University of Oklahoma, for instance, an essential feature of the original planning was the Bachelor of Liberal Studies program, a comprehensive adult learning project combining independent study and intensive residential experiences.

A creative effort of the faculty of the University of Oklahoma, the planning effort, funded by the Carnegie Corporation, began with a year-long seminar of some forty scholars representative of the entire faculty of the University. The recommendations emerging from this faculty dialogue served as guide lines for a ten-man degree committee who deliberated for three years, consulting with no less than one hundred of their colleagues, and finally produced an innovative curriculum leading to the Bachelor of Liberal Studies degree.

This curriculum takes cognizance of the fact that few adults can meet classes during the day, and many simply cannot control their time or location even to attend regularly spaced evening classes; the curriculum also recognizes that the prescriptive requirements of degree programs in most institutions—which involve enrollment in X number of curriculum fragments for X number of hours per week for four years, regardless of pre-existing experiences and learning brought to the studies—constitute barriers of both time and irrelevance, since many University courses designed for youngsters are simply irrelevant in their content and approach to the concerns of mature adults.

The B.L.S. program was designed to meet the two-fold test of availability and relevancy to adults. The curriculum consists of three broad areas: social sciences, natural sciences and humanities—each of which may be taken in any sequence—culminating with a fourth major integrative component, inter-area studies. These areas are arranged in a sequence of four courses of independent or guided study, plus four related residential seminars. The program of each adult student is based on his own capability, needs, prior learning and time available for study.

## PROGRAM INVOLVES INDEPENDENT STUDY

A student admitted to the B.L.S. program first takes about one and a half days of placement tests which are interpreted to him either in personal consultations or by letter. An advisor works with the student on developing a plan for independent study in whichever area they agree is most appropriate. The student then has an independent period to complete his studies in that area through reading, correspondence with his advisor both by mail and through the use of tape recorders, attendance at week-end "group advisement" conferences, and a comprehensive examination which involves both objective-type questions and an essay.

Following completion of independent study, with a satisfactory score on the area comprehensive examination, the student is eligible to participate in an area seminar, a three-week residential session conducted by a teaching team of at least two faculty members, plus one or more resource scholars.

When the student has completed all three areas of independent study, he plunges into the inter-area independent study phase. This consists of focusing on the integrative aspects of subject matter through the study and criticism of nine required books, the preparation of either a paper on a highly specialized subject or some appropriate creative work, and a comprehensive examination consisting of four essay questions. The test frequently consumes more than four hours and is evaluated by two readers.

The final step in the B.L.S. program is the completion of the inter-area residential seminar, four weeks long, centering on a problem or a theme of broad scope involving the application of subject matter from all three of the area studies. This seminar is an approximation of the typical graduate seminar held in a residence program.

Since the inception of the B.L.S. program in January 1961, more than one thousand students have enrolled, and by the end of the 1967–1968 academic year one hundred degrees will have been conferred. Students range in age from under twenty to over seventy-one and reside in forty-seven states, the District of Columbia, the territory of Puerto Rico and eleven foreign countries.

The success of the B.L.S. program led to the approval by the University in 1967 of a master of liberal studies degree, another precedent-shattering event since this program, too, is an independent study, intensive residential experience degree, but at the *graduate* level. It is designed primarily for persons holding bachelor's degrees in specialized disciplines such as business or engineering, but may also be pursued by former B.L.S. students.

In an effort to acquaint the local community with the philosophy objectives and facilities, Dean Thomas P. Bergin of the Notre Dame Center invited over twelve hundred individuals from representative organizations within the South Bend community to some nine "Evenings at the Center." Following the evenings at the Center, he scheduled a community development round table workshop in which seventeen agencies got together for a full day and exchanged ideas on their own responsibilities within the area and on the inter-relationship of these responsibilities among the other agencies. This type of meeting had not been held before and, according to Bergin, "proved to be tremendously beneficial to all of the various agencies involved."

Of the Center's dedicatory conference, "Theological Issues of Vatican II," Father Hesburgh, President of Notre Dame wrote: "Nothing we have done yet at Notre Dame in my almost fifteen years of Presidency has received so much attention here and abroad." He added, "The conference was absolutely spectacular and better than anyone had anticipated. It was even carried in about ten cities on the Eastern seaboard by closed circuit television, which is quite a measure of Continuing Education."

With regard to a conference on "The Role of Karl Marx in the Modern World," the *New York Times* called attention to the fact that it involved "fifteen philosophers, political scientists, historians, theologians, and sociologists from Poland, Czechoslovakia, Yugoslavia, Germany, and France as well as the United States."

A three day-session, May 8 through May 10, 1967, was an ecumenical seminar on "The Human Sciences and the Church." Of it, Bergin said, "This conference, sponsored jointly by churches and community groups with a major University, provides an opportunity for clergy and laity to learn from college and university persons themselves what is stirring on the campus in the way of new knowledge and its impact upon the world. In this context, we hope to discover ways for the churches to relate more effectively to colleges and universities, and to participate wherever possible in the great issues and movements which are shaping the future." Seven papers were presented on the behaviorial sciences in the modern world and their relation to religion.

A letter from Chalmers H. Goshorn, Jr., Pastor of the First Presbyterian Church of Jeffersonville, Indiana, said, "The seminar was a real blast of fresh air to me. It is so easy to become involved in the technicalities of local pastoral responsibilities, and the task of relating oneself and the church that one serves to the work-a-day world. It is a source of inspiration to what is otherwise barren for one to come in contact with a conference that is dealing with the searching, critical, studious issues of our time. The conference itself did much to quicken my own desire to return to scholarship that I have neglected, to engage in some penetrating soul-searching, and to be more alert to issues of mutual concern."

## NEBRASKA HALL OF YOUTH

At the University of Nebraska, the Hall of Youth, with its programs designed both for young people planning to remain in agriculture and those preparing for an urban industrial occupation, is an extension of the Continuing Education idea into the immediate post-high school years. As the remarks of one participant indicate, these short courses frequently are extremely influential. He wrote:

*"Little did I realize, when I started the Short Course, what influence it would have on me. It helped me to decide what I really wanted to do. . . .*

*"The course was very beneficial to me in several ways. First it expanded my knowledge of different types and ways of farming and ranching which are very essential today . . .*

*"I learned about new varieties of crops, and the study of agricultural economics helped me make better decisions on the ranch. . . .*

*"All these subjects, plus the various tours, helped me to decide to enroll in the college of Agriculture and Home Economics for a four-year course. I hope to expand my knowledge further and return to ranching and farming."*

However, Clinton A. Hoover, head of the Hall of Youth, is not complacent as rise the numbers of youth involved in Center programs since he believes that the University should be even more creative in its programming than in the past. "Many of our programs involve 4-H and other youth groups that could and would carry on their activities elsewhere if the Center were not here," he said. The infrequent times of the year when young people are available for Continuing Education conferences causes periods of feast and famine in the use of Center facilities. "We've not yet solved the problem of involving the non-farm youth, either," Hoover said, "but we're working on it." Among the special projects he is developing is a national program in which an outstanding high school farm-oriented junior from each state will come to the Center in the summer and, in addition to attending seminars at the Center, will spend several weeks with a Nebraska farm family to exchange experiences and ideas. Another exchange program is international, with farm youth from Japan coming to Nebraska for agricultural-related study.

The Center at the University of Oxford is a most appropriate setting for conferences involving international exchanges. One such program was the International Conference on Workers' Education held at Rewley House. Of this conference, the Secretary of the Delegacy for Extra-Mural Studies, said:

> *"'Labor educators' in the U.S.A. have long been a distinct and even separate species of adult educators. In British adult education, too, trade union education has in the past ten years been emerging as a distinctive feature.*
>
> *"Those not directly implicated in labor education often do not realize the strains on a university department trying to serve labor, management, and the community in an area of always imminent conflict and organizational jealousies and suspicion. This conference was deliberately called a 'private' one, so that individuals could be invited on a personal basis, both to ensure high quality of participants and to avoid these organizational difficulties."*

Oxford's conference planners believed that a small, "hand-picked" conference would be able to discuss freely and effectively. This belief, Jessup felt, was amply justified by results. From the U.S.A., two heads of University labor schools, a professor of adult education, and the Director of Education of the AFL/CIO, took part. From Britain there were six senior faculty members from Oxford, five members of the Delegacy's labour education staff and the Principal of Ruskin College; in addition there were two experienced tutors from other universities, a union education officer, and a national officer from one of Britain's largest unions. Although primarily an Anglo-American conference, there were also five people from the Continent of Europe—the head and member of the staff of a French University labor institute, the principal of a German trade union college, a German extra-mural tutor, and a labor educator from Denmark. Altogether there were 27 members of the conference. Most stayed for five days, but some were able to stay longer and take part in wider discussions on English adult education with the Delegacy's adult education staff.

Eight papers were submitted on (a) teaching methods, (b) the role of the university, (c) labor education and adult education, in Britain, the United States and Germany. "These," Jessup said, "formed the basis for extraordinarily fruitful and illuminating discussions, and an edited selection of the papers is to be published."

The Delegacy provided all members with a comprehensive selection of published British papers on the topic of the conference and of its own teaching materials. Members of the conference also arranged among themselves for the systematic exchange of information on programs and of teaching materials. Of the conference, Jessup said:

*"Those taking part learned a great deal, not only about each other's work and problems, but about their own. The process of self-examination and critical review of one's own practices and beliefs was clearly at work. Both the Americans and the British labor educators were made freshly aware of the importance of labor education maintaining its place in the mainstream of adult education.*

*"The strengthening of institutional links and the development of personal ones will undoubtedly follow from the conference. For all those taking part it was a memorable occasion; the quality of the participants, the papers and the discussions was high, the growth of warm personal respect and friendship was evident and everyone felt that somehow something had been started which would go on and would be of importance for labor and adult education in the U.S.A., Britain, and the Continent of Europe."*

## NOT JUST "CONFERENCE" CENTERS

Perhaps the most important thing about the Centers for Continuing Education, however, is that none of them is just a "conference" center. Although the conference activity is the most visible part of the program—as the Center, itself, is the most visible facility—the centers are actually simply the starting point for a broad range of Continuing Education activities including, in addition to the conference and institute program and its direct "outreach" phases, credit and non-credit evening classes, correspondence or independent study departments, radio and television facilities, audio-visual libraries and studios, and special programs such as off-campus classes, community development services, and units with special subject matter orientation.

Whether its name is "Continuing Education Service," "General Extension," "University Extension" or some other designation, the outreach arm of the university (and that arm is dean or director) is usually housed in the Center for Continuing Education and is responsible not only for the center program but also for the other extension activities. And the existence of a center focuses attention on the total program as well as on the conference and institute phase.

At a recent University of Oklahoma faculty gathering, the question of the effect of a center on the university, itself, was raised. The response was dramatic: "It has changed the university," one faculty member said, and around the table were nods of unanimous agreement from colleagues representing nearly every discipline of the institution. "Here at the Center we redefine our teaching goals and methods and carry them back to our main-campus classrooms," another said. A scientist said, "The Center symbolizes our responsibility to the state, the region, and the nation as well as to our campus student body, and to research." A psychologist concerned with urban problems said, "And the Center provides a focal point for people in communities all over the state; no matter where the action is, they all know it starts at the Oklahoma Center."

Thus whether it is a staff-originated conference, a faculty-inspired invitational seminar, a group-requested special program, a center-based activity, an independent-study degree sequence, or a community-wide action program, the essential fact is that it is Continuing Education in action. When a specially trained staff, headquartered in a specially designed facility, has available the rich resources of a great university and the imaginative cooperation of its faculty and administration, the potential for influence and innovation is enormous. While some creative work is clearly being done, it is also clear that the permutations are virtually infinite, the populations are universal, and course content, program design and instructional method are capable of whatever flexibility and refinement Continuing Educators can and will demand from them. The possibilities are prodigious. Results depend on the skill, sophistication and, perhaps, the serendipity of the continuing educators.

"A Continuing Education Center," H. R. Neville, Provost of Michigan State University, said, "is the University's front door to the people of the state, the nation, and the world."

# CHAPTER 5

# Improving Continuing Education: Studies and Training Programs

J. Harris Ward, then executive vice-president of the Commonwealth Edison Company, wrote in 1957:

"Today everybody is in the conference business. I cannot believe they are all doing the job well. There is reason to believe, actually, that some of them are doing it quite badly. If the execution of these programs in Continuing Education is bad, their effectiveness will be threatened just as definitely as if the educational substance were poor.

"It seems to me that it would be extremely beneficial to study at the graduate level all aspects of Continuing Education at conference centers. The success of existing conference centers suggests that they should exist in greater numbers and it seems that they almost certainly will. It seems to me also that the time has come to find out who is performing the job of Continuing Education well, and why. So far as I know this is not being done today, and such a project would represent a contribution of national importance."

Ward's statement was designed to support the proposal of Professor Cyril O. Houle that a studies and training program be made part of the activities facilitated by the Kellogg Foundation grant to the University of Chicago for a Center for Continuing Education. With the approval of the grant—and a similar one to the University of Nebraska—studies and training became the third distinctive contribution of the Kellogg-assisted Centers for Continuing Education. (The first two contributions were a specially designed facility and the team concept of program planning and presentation.)

Of his proposal, Professor Houle said:

"The fundamental assumption which underlies the program of studies and training is that if Continuing Education is to develop soundly and constructively, it must do so on the basis of tested knowledge and under the direction of men and women adequately prepared to undertake their responsibilities.

"While Continuing Education is becoming a major factor in American

92

higher education, it is still so new that its full scope is seldom recognized, even on those campuses where conference programs have been most fully developed. And yet, as with any other institution, patterns of behavior and response gradually build up into tradition. As the number of centers grows to perhaps a hundred or more, practices will freeze into patterns, and images will become increasingly difficult to change."

Essentially, Professor Houle (who has in preparation a two-volume work dealing systematically with the whole field of adult education) felt that programs of Continuing Education must, of necessity, be guided by men and women of stature and competence who would be able to speak as university staff members and who would have resources to carry out their ideas and convictions. He stressed that Continuing Education programs should be carefully examined to develop concrete and realistic data about the process and practice of continuing education in order to improve its activities. Among the essentials for excellence are:

(1) The clear commitment of university boards of trustees, administrators, and faculty to the concept that Continuing Education is an essential responsibility of the university;

The Library at the Nebraska Center for Continuing Education contains basic reference works on its shelves. For special needs of conferences, the Library can be stocked with books of varied nature obtained from the various libraries of the university.

(2) The careful design of objectives and structure to achieve high-level educational purposes, reflects the many facets of the university's competence, and has the maximum possible educational impact; and

(3) The immediate and ultimate effect of contributing to the university as well as to the conference participants.

Professor Houle pointed out that Continuing Education centers could be used effectively as laboratories for social and behavioral research. He said, "The Center brings to the University a large number of men and women of various ages and social conditions. They participate in many different kinds of activities, most of which can be observed and otherwise studied, and, with permission, recorded. Conference participa ts usually have spare time between conference sessions, and the majority of these adults would be delighted to be involved in any program of study which appeared sensible to them."

A studies and training program in Continuing Education, it has been suggested, might concentrate on the involvement and education of future leaders and practitioners who would be concerned about evaluation and improvement and would be able, because of their training and participation, to make Continuing Education a fundamental part of the total educational matrix of the modern world.

## INTERNSHIP PROGRAMS

The internship programs at the University of Nebraska and the University of Chicago were steps in this direction. The internship programs are a combination of intensive graduate study in adult education and a planned and supervised conference work experience in the universities' Centers for Continuing Education.

The pattern of the internship remains flexible to the individual and program needs. The general pattern of the internship calls for the student to devote six months in full-time theoretical study (generally aimed at meeting requirements for the M.A. or Ph.D. degree) and six months in a combination of two-thirds supervised "real-life" work and one-third theoretical study. During the six months practical work, the intern is a member of the staff of the Center while also receiving faculty instruction, counseling, and interpretation from the Director of Studies and Training. The intern receives four graduate credits for his six months of practical experience.

One intern's schedule of responsibilities at the University of Chicago involved work on six conferences selected to provide a graded sequence of experiences. The first three conferences were conducted by the intern in conjunction with experienced coordinators who gradually turned over more responsibility to the intern. These conferences exposed him to different coordinators and to content material increasingly removed from his area of competence. Next came three conferences for which the intern alone was responsible. The final experience of this internship was full involvement with the Dean of University Extension in a major endeavor, "The China Conference," in which planning and execution of a extremely demanding nature was required. The "China Conference" received much well-deserved praise. Subsequent to his internship, this young intern was employed by the Dean to help plan and execute another conference initiated by the Center: "Man as a Hunter."

Learning experiences were not confined to the Center itself. One intern worked with an adult education professor on a conference program sponsored by the Adult Education Council of Greater Chicago; another worked on plans for the Adult Education Association of the U.S.A. annual meeting in Chicago in November; a third intern worked on program planning for a workshop for administrators of public school adult education.

These interns met every other week as a group with the Director of Studies and Training, developed a program of reading or research, visited other facilities, and attended professional meetings such as The Residential Section Meetings of the Adult Education Association of the U.S.A., the National Seminar on Adult Education Research, and the Conference and Institute Section meetings of the National University Extension Association.

Each intern maintained a daily diary during the entire period of his work experience, had a weekly interview with the Director of Studies and Training, and had regular consultations with the Coordinator of Interns, the Center Program Director and the Center Business Manager.

At Nebraska the internship program, supported also by the Kellogg Foundation, was similar to that at Chicago. In 1966–1967 one intern, a public school adult educator from New York, spent his first six months in full-time study and the second six months in full-time conference coordination. Asked whether his internship in a residential setting would have any value to him as administrator of a non-residential continuing education program, he said, "Of course, it will! The program planning cycle and techniques of instruction I've learned here will be useful anywhere. And the idea of concentrated longer periods of contact is something I can build into my program by having four or five hour meetings on a half dozen Saturdays, say, rather than one hour a week for eighteen or twenty weeks."

While Michigan State University does not have a Kellogg Foundation-financed internship program, a few students pursuing graduate degrees in adult education may receive internships for which they involve themselves in study and training at the Kellogg Center for approximately twenty hours a week for the full school year. A three-credit tutorial course taught by members of the Center staff, and covering a broad range of subjects from "Philosophical relationships between Continuing Education and the total University" to "Publicity and Promotion," is combined with observation of conference planning and presentation during the fall and winter terms, and the total responsibility for four conferences during spring term.

## RESEARCH

A number of research projects have been developed as part of the Kellogg Foundation-assisted studies and training programs. Interns and research assistants work with the major staff members in the conduct of basic studies. In addition, the interns propose studies of their own, usually in connection with their theses. Some are highly practical studies aimed at the specific improvement of performance of conference centers and programs through the development of longer conferences, the building of programs around broad social, civic, and cultural themes, the definition of new target audiences and demonstration of how they may be reached, and the filling of awkward times on the schedule. Some are fundamental and theoretical.

A study of the pattern of organization, the institutional flexibility, and the demonstration potential of the five original Kellogg centers is under way at the University of Chicago. Among other studies under way or completed at the University are the following:

1. The Influence of Pre-Conference Study on Learning During the Conference Period.

2. Guidelines for Planning and Executing University Continuing Education Center Programs—Theory and Practice.

3. A National Survey of Residential Centers for Continuing Education.

4. The History of Residential Continuing Education.

5. Program Planning and Program Effectiveness in University Residential Centers.

6. The Development and Testing of a Typology of University Residential Adult Education Programs.

One of the most valuable potential contributions of Centers for Continuing Education is their use for studies of a fundamental sort. At the University of Chicago, for example, Professor Herbert Thelen and six research assistants tested some hypotheses about what combinations of persons will result in effective operation of small groups. An attempt was made to *predict* the behavior of groups constituted in various ways rather than merely *describe* behavior after it had occurred. Using the data obtained, the kinds of small group experiences that would be influenced most or least by group composition could be predicted, and information useful to conference planners on how to set up experiences so groups could understand and learn most effectively was also obtained. An unplanned effect of this study was that the associations which sponsored the several conferences which were studied have begun to adapt their methods based on the study conclusions.

The measurement and analysis of the total extent of an adult's participation in educational activities were undertaken in a study by Dr. Ann Litchfield, Director of Studies and Training in Continuing Education at Chicago. The instrument developed in this study, plus the avenues of inquiry opened by the investigation, suggest basic ways to achieve better understanding of the clientele of adult education as well as methods which will place the residential conference experience within the context of the total of an individual's efforts to learn.

Utilizing student records of those who have been participants at the Center for Continuing Education at the University of Oklahoma, Mr. Warren Abraham of Miami University (Ohio), is examining the implications of changes in the life cycle of the adult student on his interest in participation.

With these studies, and those being undertaken in centers across the country, the dessemination of the tested knowledge and opinion in Continuing Education is an extremely important aspect of the Studies and Training Program. As one way of achieving this purpose *The Continuing Education Report* has been published as good material becomes available. Some of the titles are the following:

"What is Continuing Education?" Cyril O. Houle, University of Chicago.

"The Conference Coordinator: Educator Or Facilitator?" Chester W. Leathers, Georgia Center for Continuing Education, and William S. Griffith, University of Chicago.

"Oxford University and Adult Education," Frank Jessup, University of Oxford.

"The School for Life," N.F.S. Grundtvig, Titular Bishop, Danish Lutheran Church, and Harold J. Alford, University of Minnesota.

"The Director of Conference Programming: His Attitudes Toward Job Role," Donald A. Deppe, University of Maryland.

"Is University Faculty Committed to Conference Programs?" Tunis H. Decker, Michigan State University.

"Residential Program Data: A Statistical Description," Lawrence E. Devlin and Ann Litchfield, University of Chicago.

## IN-SERVICE TRAINING

But even with the spread of formal training in doctoral programs and the development of internships—providing both professional personnel and, through their research, a growing body of knowledge about the field—the need for competent, knowledgeable people to operate the Continuing Education enterprise continues to outstrip the supply so that, as Dr. J. E. Burkett,

Assistant Dean at the University of Oklahoma, put it, "The continued recruitment of new program specialists and of specialized employees in service units increases the need for implementation of the program of employee orientation and in-service training."

Dean Thomas Bergin of the University of Notre Dame echoed the same plaint in his first annual report:

*"As I visited the various Centers and talked with people involved in Continuing Education programs throughout the United States, I made arrangements to interview those promising young people who are working for their doctoral degree in Continuing Education. Because the entire field is expanding so rapidly, there is no great pool of capable and responsible people to draw upon. For the most part, existing centers have found the necessary faculty resources through their existing University Extension operations and have trained their own people for coordinating work. Because Notre Dame does not have an Extension program, it was necessary to do a great deal of searching. After a vast number of interviews, we were, indeed, fortunate in being able to secure two first-rate faculty additions to the staff."*

Chester W. Leathers, a conference coordinator at the Georgia Center, who had a Chicago internship while working toward his master's degree, returned

There are no "drop-outs" or "sleepers-in" at the pictured Georgia Center conference.

to Georgia in 1965 as supervisor of coordinators and wrote Dr. Litchfield to say:

*"One of my goals as Supervisor of the Department of Conferences is to help our staff develop a 'philosophy of coordination.' To do this we have had to begin with basic fundamentals: what is 'Continuing Education,' why residential conference centers, why the Georgia Center, etc.*

*"Our staff (eight coordinators, two assistant coordinators, and the supervisor) is presently studying 'the program planning process.' Each coordinator leads a discussion on the planning process of a conference which he coordinated in the past few months. The group attempts to 'reconstruct,' step by step, the planning and execution of the conference. We meet almost each week and the results so far are, I think, wonderful.*

*"As a change of pace for these sessions, we invite a Center staff member from another department (e.g., Food Service, Library Services, Communications, Audio-Visuals, Housekeeping, etc.) to discuss that department's function in the overall operation of the Center. It seems to me that we are really gaining a better understanding of how each department functions and how we all work together towards the same 'ends,' and we learn more about each other as individual personalities.*

*"Another interesting development, I think, is our Staff Seminar. About sixteen members of our staff in the Instructional Division meet every other Friday morning for a breakfast discussion period.*

*"For ten weeks we discussed the 'Great Decisions' (Foreign Policy) and now we are discussing the 'Basic Issues of Man,' a liberal studies program designed and developed by the University of Georgia College of Arts and Sciences, and the Georgia Center. This seminar was developed voluntarily and the enthusiasm displayed by the individual members is tremendous."*

At Michigan State University, Tunis Dekker, Director of Conferences, who received his doctorate from the University of Chicago, also has a coordinator in-service training program involving discussion of "The Ways of Mankind," as well as more practical day-to-day problems.

Recently, opportunities for professional development have been developed outside individual institutional in-service training programs. Michigan State University and the University of Chicago both offer residential seminars for University adult education: Michigan State for four days in mid-winter, Chicago for three weeks in mid-summer. Of the 1966 Chicago workshop, Dr. Ann Litchfield wrote:

"The program of lectures, discussion, self-directed individual study, and thought provoking exchanges between participants, who represent a variety of university adult education activities, is designed to stimulate professional growth. In each of the nine years of the workshop attention has been given to Continuing Education, but this topic became a central theme in 1963 and for each subsequent year of the workshop, including 1966, which had, as one of four major objectives to encourage the investigation of theoretical and practical approaches to residential Continuing Education. The following major addresses dealt directly with residential continuing education:

*Creating a Climate for Learning* by Hugh Masters, Director of the Georgia Center for Continuing Education, The University of Georgia.

*History of Residential Continuing Education* by Harold J. Alford, Associate Professor and Director, The Department of Off-Campus Classes, University of Minnesota.

*Staff Selection and Training and Retention in Residential Centers for Continuing Education* by Ann Litchfield, Assistant Professor, University of Chicago, and Director of the Studies and Training Program in Continuing Education.

*An Appraisal of the Kellogg Centers for Continuing Education—Their Role in Adult Education* by William Griffith, Chairman of the Adult Education Committee, the University of Chicago.

*The Effects of Setting upon the Education Achievement of Adults* by James Lahr, Associate Dean of University College, Washington University at St. Louis."

The advantages of "learning-in-residence" were capitalized upon during the 1966 workshop. Most of the twenty-seven participants lived in the Center for Continuing Education. Brice Ratchford, Vice President for Extension, University of Missouri, also lived in the Center and served as a tutor-in-residence, holding conferences and buzz sessions in the Center suite provided for that purpose. Ross Waller, Professor, Department of Adult Education at the University of Manchester, England, and Head of Holly Royde Residential Center (who joined the workshop for the third week) also served as a focal point for many informal learning sessions.

The Conference and Institute section of the National University Extension Association (NUEA) and the Residential section of the Adult Education Association of the U.S.A. provide places where continuing education practitioners can meet to discuss mutual problems and concerns. The NUEA group also has begun to sponsor regular pre-conference workshops where particular problems can be pursued in depth. A new phase of their program of in-service training—regional workshops—was started in 1967 at the University of Georgia. Of this development the committee wrote:

*"The professional development committee of the Curriculum and Instruction (C. & I.) Division of NUEA assumes that there are two basic models of devel-*

*opment of C. & I. personnel: the professional model and the craft model. The professional model emphasizes philosophical and theoretical concerns. The craft model emphasizes "functional elements" which are part of the operational concerns of the job. The pre-conference program of the C. & I. Division has emerged as primarily of the professional model. This emphasis will be maintained in the future. The new regional workshop program will be primarily of the craft model. the annual pre-conference program will attempt to develop an amalgam of professional and craft which will be of interest and value to both experienced and inexperienced personnel. The regional workshops will be geared primarily to the inexperienced. Accordingly, the Committee has planned a workshop for the following purpose:*

> *. . . to help the participant improve his skills in planning and conducting conferences.*

*The objectives of the workshop are directed toward:*
> *. . . developing or refining principles of conference*
> *planning and execution . . . applying these principles to practice.*

*The workshop staff will be made up of people with years of extensive experience in C. & I. programs of all types and characteristics. Members of the C. & I. Professional Development Committee will play key instructional and consultative roles in this program."*

## OXFORD UNIVERSITY'S ROLE

Part of the Kellogg Foundation grant to the University of Oxford provides a stipend and expense money each year to permit a leader of American Continuing Education to visit England for two months as a "Kellogg Fellow." The first three were Charles Wedemeyer of the University of Wisconsin in 1965, Thurman White of the University of Oklahoma in 1966, and Paul Sheats of the University of California in 1967. Of his experience, Wedemeyer wrote:

*"The Kellogg Fellowship at Oxford University is significant not only for what it is; it is significant for what it is not. It is significant because it is the first such fellowship open to American adult educators. Consequently it should be looked upon as an innovative device in the broad attempt to improve the quality and breadth of training for adult educators. The success of the Kellogg Fellowship (at least from my point of view) suggests that we ought to have in the United States similar hosts to which we can invite distinguished colleagues from other countries. The value to us as hosts and to our visiting colleagues is in many respects immeasurable, for the value is personal as well as professional."*

Both Wedemeyer and White comment on the fact that the program was set up so they could do what they wanted to do: lecture at Oxford and other universities, with Mr. Jessup and his staff making whatever arrangements were necessary; observe and participate in the adult education activities carried on at Rewley House and at other institutions; study in the excellent libraries of Oxford University; read, reflect, write; talk with cultivated Britains about the problems of education. "I could," Wedemeyer said, "to the extent possible in the time that was at my disposal, try to get inside the British academic community and understand it in a way that the transient visitor cannot." Both he and White also travelled to other communities in Britain to observe the many variants of adult education carried on in the island.

Wedemeyer concluded:

*"Friendships grew under the influence of sometimes warm discussions whose give and take left few topics untouched. In all these encounters with the British I had to reach—reach far back in my knowledge of English literature and English history for the anecdotes and the quotations and the factual information that would illustrate a point or demonstrate a conviction. I had to think of ways of describing adult education at my own institution and elsewhere in the United States that would make reasonable sense to those who had not participated in the historical development of these activities. I had to look again and again at the American society from which I had come and attempt to assess it and evaluate it. I had to think introspectively of my own role in adult education and what my institution was doing and critically examine many of the things that I had long taken for granted as 'givens' in our condition or as 'goods' which now, under the stimulus of a new environment, were called into question. I had to ask questions, framing them so that they would convey to my listener a sense of the intellectual excitement which I felt at Oxford. I had to think through American policy in many political areas so that I could discuss these without undue emotion or bias but with some objectivity and intellectual depth."*

Wedemeyer and White participated in the planning and presentation of special conferences at Rewley House. They found that the conferences and seminars at Rewley House were carefully prepared, with working papers submitted in advance to all of the participants. Of this Wedemeyer said, "What seemed to me a high proportion of students came with some advance preparation completed." Wedemeyer observed that the organizing tutor (the person in charge of the particular activity) did not always act as the moderator of the discussion or debate. Nevertheless, the organizing tutor made known in many ways his responsibility and concern for the general progress of the discussions. Wedemeyer said, "The tutors work together as a team,

University-oriented adult education is very much the order of the day in England. The pictured conference is one of many held at the Oxford Centre during a school year.

probing and stimulating each other and the students into sharpened analyses of the issues and the materials." He noted that the tutors met together regularly during the course of conferences to assess what was happening, discuss changes of roles, introduce new elements that were necessary because of the progress or lack of progress being made, and generally evaluate what was going on.

Of the participants, Wedemeyer said:

*"The students whom I got to know in several Rewley House conferences were, as they are in the United States, a varied lot. Some were from the professions, some were housewives, some were teachers, some were students in training, some were young, some middle aged, some elderly. They tended to come from a wide range of backgrounds and standards, although they were a much more homogeneous group than is characteristic of much that we describe as adult or extension education. Adult education in Britain, by and large, is an activity aimed at an elite in the British society. I do not mean an economic elite or a social elite; I mean an intellectual elite. There were, of course, varied degrees of formal education represented in the groups which admitted me as a participant. What struck me most, however, was that in the discussions and debates which characterized the Rewley House conferences, the degree of formal education completed seemed hardly at all related to the degree of intelligent participation offered by the students."*

Wedemeyer was particularly impressed with the way that the residential situation of the conferences, seminars, and meetings proved to be a definite stimulus to the generation of identification with Rewley House and Oxford University, with the development of friendships between students and tutors, and with the clarification of goals and purposes which drew students together. "The Common Room and the Dining Room," he said, "are as important in this kind of adult education as the class or seminar room." White stressed that Oxford University and the Town of Oxford are almost synonymous, with the several colleges and the town shops all part of a single community, so that Oxford swiftly became a way of life, and even outside Rewley House one felt still involved in a total educational experience.

One particular Oxford conference, an "Anglo-American Conference on University Adult Education" at Rewley House, provided further international exchanges in the interest of increasing understanding and improving practices. There were 52 participants: twenty-four from the United States, ten from Canada, two from Hong Kong, one from Singapore, and fifteen from England, Wales and Scotland. The conference was regarded in part as a "curtain raiser" to the much larger and wider conference of the International Congress of University Adult Education to be held in Denmark the following week. However, the main purpose of the conference was to give an opportunity for a comparatively small and homogeneous group of university adult educators in North America and Britain to meet, discuss their respective theories, practices, and problems in university adult education, and to consider possible means of Anglo-American cooperation in this field. The Oxford conference, according to Frank Jessup, showed how much can be achieved in a few days where there are no language problems and where, in spite of differences of theory and practice, the background and fundamental assumptions are common to all the participants.

KELLOGG-ASSISTED CENTERS SHARE DATA

In April 1962 representatives of the then five Kellogg-supported centers met at the University of Nebraska to discuss mutual concerns and agreed to collect and share data on programs held at each of the centers. The study design and collection supervision and analysis were performed at the University of Chicago Center for Continuing Education through its Kellogg Foundation grant. Broadened to include ten centers (five not Kellogg Foundation-assisted) the committee met at the University of Chicago in December 1966, and approved release of a report and voted to continue the study for several years.

Among other things, this data-sharing program revealed that, contrary to some fears, programs at the centers were not huge unwieldly affairs; the

1967 analysis showed that more than half had fewer than fifty participants. By far the greatest percentage—more than 80%—were conferences, a category of program involving the use of the facilities when the Continuing Education staff took full or joint responsibility for the education and welfare of the people occupying and using the center's facilities. Almost 7% of the facilities' use was for credit or non-credit courses of several sessions, with intervals of two or more days between sessions, whereas almost 10% of the events involved the use of the facility to accommodate sequential programs, usually a series of sessions prescribed for a single group within one year.

Although fewer than 50% of the programs lasted for two days or less, 35%, five days or longer, almost 10% lasted more than two weeks. About half of the programs were sponsored by the University alone or in cooperation with some external audience, whereas the other half involved the use of the facilities by an external group either for its own membership or for the general public.

More than 80% of the events were occupation-related; however, more than 10% directly focused on social responsibility. One aspect of continuity indicated by the data from the centers was that more than 60% of the programs were repeated or expanded from previous years and almost half were regional or national or international in scope as judged from the home base of participants and staff.

## MORE TRAINING AND RESEARCH NEEDED

Thus, data collection and sharing, in-service training, and professional meetings held locally, regionally, nationally, and internationally, and formal university graduate studies, training, and research programs have been stimulated by the Kellogg Foundation-assisted Centers for Continuing Education. Yet training and research remain two of the activities urgently needing further development. Most centers still do not have clearly defined staff in-service training programs, and program evaluation is usually confined to a "reaction inventory" of some sort, solicited with varying degrees of persistence from conference participants.

At the Notre Dame Center, for example, the reaction inventory consists of a simple mimeographed sheet handed to each participant. It asks him to circle a simple "yes," "undecided," or "no" answer to about eleven questions ranging from whether he received sufficient advance information about the program to whether or not he would recommend this program for another similar group. Some of the concerns are with the physical accommodations—registration, lodging, eating—while others involve the emphasis, balance, and variety of topics, opportunity for informal conversations, and whether or not the program ran smoothly. In addition, the Notre

Dame questionnaire asks the participant to rate the conference by checking his reactions on a scale ranging from "It was one of the most rewarding experiences I ever had" to "I am not taking any new ideas away." There is also space for open-ended comments or suggestions.

An evaluation division was one of the original major areas of administration at the University of Georgia, but it was discontinued. This was because the problems in developing program had to take precedence over a research activity. Also the locating of an individual qualified by background and interest in evaluation and research proved most difficult and when the original evaluation director moved on, he simply was not replaced.

A year prior to the opening of the Nebraska Center, Allan Knox, professor of adult education and director of research, initiated baseline studies of the adult population of the state of Nebraska and its patterns of participation in adult education. Knox left Nebraska for Columbia University, however, and the studies he started have not been materially built upon.

But as increasing numbers of Continuing Education administrators with graduate degrees in adult education take over positions of leadership in major university programs, evaluation methods, research projects, staff training programs and "continuing education of continuing educators" also increases. Harris Ward's objective of finding out who is doing the Continuing Education job well, and why, is one goal; improving the practice of Continuing Education in the light of such findings is another.

CHAPTER 6

# Keeping the House Full and in the Black: Administration and Finance

On the university president's desk were two letters. One was from the director of extension, the other from the business vice-president. The extension director wrote:

*"It is very clear that on the one hand this building will be a service enterprise. Someone will have to be in charge of renting rooms, providing meals, running the garage, employing cooks, maids and housekeepers, and the efficient operation of what will amount to a dormitory enterprise. On the other hand, the building will house an educational enterprise the success of which will be sole justification for the erection of the building. Clearly that part of the work must be done by a trained educator who is also endowed with certain gifts in the way of administration and ability to make contacts. The laying out of a program to keep the building busy with groups of various kinds throughout the year will be a full-time job of the greatest importance."*

The vice-president for business wrote:

*"I have felt that there were two quite distinct phases of activities to be carried on in the building. One phase would be the activity carried on by, say, the Director of Adult Education. This individual would be responsible for contacting professional groups, arranging for courses of study, making the necessary arrangements with members of the staff for lectures, etc. With this phase, of course, my office is not concerned. The other phase is the problem of operating the building, comprising all of the duties which are ordinarily involved in operating a small hotel. It seemed to me that if the Adult Education project was to be a success the Director of Adult Education should not concern himself with the building operations of this kind."*

The year was 1936 and the president was Lotus Coffman of the University of Minnesota. The building was the University's Center for Continuation

A Center for Continuing Education is a complex enterprise, combining the financial hazards of an educational, hotel, and restaurant operation. The modern, fully equipped kitchen of the Chicago Center serves more than 500 meals on an average day.

Study, first specially designed on-campus residential center for adult study. The question posed is still the single most perplexing problem in the operation of Centers for Continuing Education: the relationship between the business staff and the program staff.

Coffman had no hesitation in making his decision. He wrote:

"I am perfectly clear that there can be no divided responsibility in the administration of the Adult Education Building. The person in charge of the dining room, the housekeeping, and every other detail of management of the building, must, in my opinion, be under the general direction of the Director."

President Coffman, however, died before his concept was put into action. Subsequent administrations permitted a division between the program director and the housekeeping director, the latter remaining under university services rather than academic administration. And when the first Kellogg-assisted Center for Continuing Education was established at Michigan State University in 1951, the division was perpetuated, since basic to the university's proposal was making the housekeeping function part of the training program of the Hotel Administration School.

The hard fact is that a Center for Continuing Education is a complex enterprise, combining the financial hazards of a hotel and restaurant operation (the latter accounting for more business failures annually than any other entrepreneurship) and education, an activity normally subsidized almost totally when provided for children and for which the college student expects to be charged one-third or less of the actual expense.

## STAFF ORGANIZATION

Operation of the Continuing Education enterprise, from maintenance through program, is a major undertaking involving a large and heterogeneous staff. At Michigan State University, for instance, the staff of the Continuing Education Service—the program arm—consists of 130 persons at the professional level, not including secretarial and clerical personnel; operating personnel for the Center facility itself—that is, personnel involved in food, housekeeping, and plant services—number 117, plus 136 part-time students. At the University of Georgia, there are approximately 500 individuals responsible to the Director of Continuing Education, from dining room waitresses to participating faculty.

Organization of the staff to provide flexible, frictionless, educationally and financially effective service is a continuing concern, and each Center has its

Maintenance is no small item in buildings so large as those housing Centers of Continuing Education.

Good food and service
are important items in
the lives of adult stu-
dents.

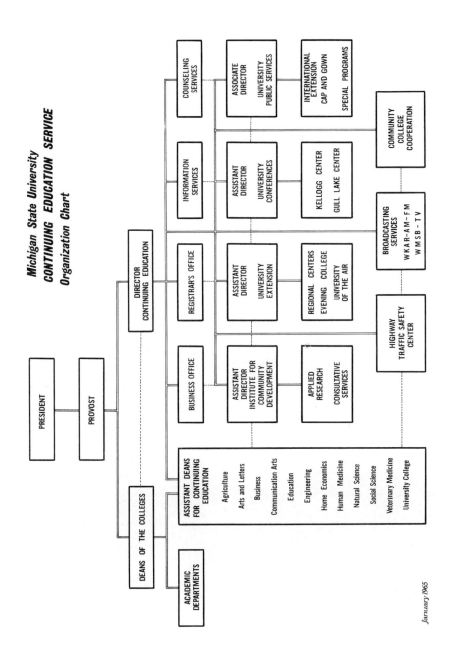

**Michigan State University**
*CONTINUING EDUCATION SERVICE*
*Organization Chart*

PRESIDENT

PROVOST

DEANS OF THE COLLEGES

ACADEMIC DEPARTMENTS

DIRECTOR CONTINUING EDUCATION

ASSISTANT DEANS FOR CONTINUING EDUCATION

Agriculture
Arts and Letters
Business
Communication Arts
Education
Engineering
Home Economics
Human Medicine
Natural Science
Social Science
Veterinary Medicine
University College

BUSINESS OFFICE

ASSISTANT DIRECTOR INSTITUTE FOR COMMUNITY DEVELOPMENT

APPLIED RESEARCH
CONSULTATIVE SERVICES

REGISTRAR'S OFFICE

ASSISTANT DIRECTOR UNIVERSITY EXTENSION

REGIONAL CENTERS EVENING COLLEGE
UNIVERSITY OF THE AIR

INFORMATION SERVICES

ASSISTANT DIRECTOR UNIVERSITY CONFERENCES

KELLOGG CENTER
GULL LAKE CENTER

COUNSELING SERVICES

ASSOCIATE DIRECTOR UNIVERSITY PUBLIC SERVICES

INTERNATIONAL EXTENSION
CAP AND GOWN
SPECIAL PROGRAMS

HIGHWAY TRAFFIC SAFETY CENTER

BROADCASTING SERVICES WKAR-AM-FM WMSB-TV

COMMUNITY COLLEGE COOPERATION

*January 1965*

111

own variations, based on institutional patterns, personnel and philosophy. Two extraordinarily successful yet quite different organizational structures are those at Georgia and Oklahoma. There is an essential similarity, however, in that both centers have a single strong and innovative leader responsible for the total operation. Another similarity, a physical one, is that the director's top assistants—those responsible for plant and program—are all officed in close proximity so that each has easy and immediate access to the others and to the director, and all take advantage of informal, personal communication opportunities.

The essential differences in the Georgia and Oklahoma organizations are that Georgia's is generalist-structured and method-oriented while Oklahoma's is specialist-structured and client-oriented, that is, each program coordinator at Georgia works with faculty and participants in many subjects but usually specializes in one method: conferences and institutes, class instruction, radio or television. At Oklahoma the coordinator is, himself, a subject matter specialist who uses a variety of methods to reach a specific clientele: management, engineers, educators, liberal studies students; the specialist frequently teaches in the courses he is coordinating. Another

Comfortable in a Georgia Center residential room are this man and wife team of conference participants. Room decor is periodically modernized and radio and/or television are standard equipment.

difference—physical—is in the center facilities, themselves, Georgia's being a single unit, Oklahoma's a complex of buildings.

At Georgia the Director of Continuing Education has three co-equal associate directors, one for instructional services, another for communications, and a third in charge of managerial services. The responsibility of the associate directors applies not only to the Center facility operation but also to the total Continuing Education program, involving on- and off-campus adult classes, correspondence study, and community services, as well as the conference and institute programs.

At Oklahoma the Dean of Continuing Education has three assistant deans, one for school and community services, one for business and industry, and a third for the College of Continuing Education which administers the Bachelor of Liberal Studies program; in addition, there is a Center manager, responsible directly to the Dean for the operation of all the center facilities.

The Director of the Managerial Services Division at Georgia is an individual who came up through the instructional services operation, so that he thoroughly understands program needs and is completely dedicated to the concept that the facility and all of its maintenance and service personnel are part of the teaching team. His overriding objective as the person in charge of managerial services is to assist the instructional divisions in accomplishing their educational mission through the smooth functioning of personnel, equipment, and the provision of a sound financial base for program operation and development.

At Oklahoma, Dean White said, "We employed a Center manager who has thirty years of successful hotel management at top level of responsibility. In order to attract him we made an administrative shift so that he is now responsible to me for the clearly defined and delimited management of housing, food, and the physical set-up of the Forum building—and that's all."

At Georgia the program departments schedule their own use of instructional facilities in cooperation with the managerial services staff. At Oklahoma the program coordinators say, "We like to think of it as buying space for our programs from the hotel management."

Physically, philosophically, and organizationally, the Georgia and Oklahoma operations differ materially, but both are financially and educationally successful and their staffs exhibit high morale, productiveness, and creativity. Clearly the team spirit of operation prevails at both Centers. At Georgia the team spirit was developed and maintained by constant vigilance and total dedication on the part of the director and his associates, with a remarkable absence of hard lines of authority. Although the conference coordinators report administratively to the associate director for instruction, it is clear that they cannot effectively plan or execute a program without involving room assignments, food services, housekeeping tasks, and publications, all of whose directors report to the associate director for management services. Similarly, it is unlikely that any of the conference coordinators would attempt to devise a conference without recourse to the audio-visual section, and frequently to the radio and television sections, all of whom report administratively to the associate director for communications. Thus, if a conference or institute is to be developed and presented effectively, the people in the various divisions, reporting administratively to the separate associate directors, have to consider themselves as part of a single team whose objective is the smooth and efficient development of an educational program; each individual team member's function is to enhance the learning process rather than simply keep an accurate set of records or insure that the snack bar makes a profit.

At Oklahoma the lines of authority are more sharply drawn than at Georgia, but the concept of service permeates the place, so that when a coordinator "buys" space for his conference from the hotel management, he gets more than space, he gets a custodial crew poised to provide for the needs of faculty and students on verbal request, and the operation moves forward smoothly with an almost total absence of multi-copy paperwork. In the Forum—the conference room building—there is a manager on duty at a very visible desk in the lobby whenever a conference is in session; with a crew of student help standing by, he is ready to move tables, chairs, movie screens or coffee service as last minute changes may demand.

A recent report of the North Central Accrediting Association—official inspection agency for Midwest colleges and universities—commended Oklahoma for the "dynamic quality of the leadership in the extension division" and for "the extent to which genuine faculty interest is expressed in its programs." The report went on: "Considering the apathy of faculties which is all too general toward extension work, the latter characteristic stands out as a major achievement, undoubtably attributable, at least in part, to the former."

## KEEPING THE HOUSE FULL

But even with sound organization, dynamic leadership, learning-centered orientation, cooperative staff interaction, and innovative programming, the maintenance of the Continuing Education facility, the salaries of operational and program coordinating staff, and the actual expenses involved in the program, itself, have to be paid for. For the most part, in present practice, this payment is derived from fees paid by program participants.

Edgar Harden, director of Continuing Education at Michigan State in 1954, said, "We earn three out of every four dollars which are expended." Later analyses showed that the Kellogg Center dining facilities and hotel rooms more than paid their own way but the program departments themselves operated at a loss.

Similar income analyses at the Georgia Center also indicated that the income from the auxiliary enterprises was substantially more than expenses. (These auxiliary earnings, as a matter of fact, accounted for most of the surplus which was accrued to finance the building of the 1966 addition.)

Because the auxiliary services—food and lodging—are both the greatest source of income and greatest source of expense for Continuing Education Centers, a basic concern of all directors is "keeping the house full." In addition to the purely monetary concern relating to occupancy, more university administrations see the Center facility as appropriately serving the university in a number of ways. First priority is, of course, given to Continuing Education activities stimulated jointly by Center staff, university faculty and community. Occupancy of the facility, however, when not scheduled for Continuing Education events is also made available for other university related activities such as the housing of transient university guests—visiting faculty, public officials, parents and relatives of students, and participants in such activities as drama festivals, high school band contests, and so on—in addition to faculty and staff meetings within the university. A third priority is usually assigned to educationally oriented community activity. At the Michigan State University Kellogg Center, for instance, 307 conferences were developed and presented during 1966 through the conference and institute staff. At the same time, 527 educational meetings were held, these being sessions ranging from the meeting of the Gladiolus Society to a session of the Council of State College Presidents. Although more meetings than conferences were held, there were 46,270 conference registrants and only 6983 meeting attendees. Another indication of the fact that educational conferences are the major activity is contained in the statistic that there were twice as many (1353) conference-days in the year as meeting-days (609).

Nonetheless, the use of centers for other than strictly educational events concerns both university administrators and outside businessmen. During the planning of the Oklahoma Center, for example, the Foundation received a telegram from the president of the Oklahoma Hotel Association saying, "We urge you to stipulate in the grant that the bedroom and dining facilities be restricted to those enrolled and participating in the seminars. We do not feel that the facilities provided in the Center should be available to any others. If the Center is provided with adequate protection to all units of free enterprise, the Center could and would provide a keen and renewed interest in seminars for adult education."

Emory Morris, President of the Foundation, replied, "I have a real appreciation for the questions raised in your telegram. At one time in my career, I had the responsibility of operating a 100-room hotel for five years. It was a delightful experience and one which I have always valued." He added, "In the proposal that we have received from the University they have assured us that if we do approve their request, the facilities developed will not be available for non-university transients."

As a matter of fact, the presence of the centers, rather than providing competition for commercial hotels and motels, has usually stimulated overnight campus visits so that in the college towns of Norman, Oklahoma, and Athens, Georgia, as well as in other Center communities, a number of new modern motels have gone into successful operation subsequent to the opening of the Centers.

The concern of educators regarding peripheral use of the facilities has to do principally with quality and image. The Oklahoma Dean said, "One of the problems we have not resolved to our satisfaction is how to incorporate 'package programs' into our curriculum development. The Center is a very attractive facility for volunteer associations, government agencies, professional organizations, and others with their own educational programs. We are quite happy to have them use the Center, but we are unhappy that we have thus far failed to find a way to incorporate them into the concept of a continuing curriculum for members of the adult student body."

In discussions at the University of Chicago, the vice-chancellor said, "We must aim at the highest quality," but he felt it was better to have lower priority meetings on occasions when the alternative was a practically empty building. "Is there anything wrong with philosophers and real estate appraisers being under the same roof?" another member of the staff asked. Agreement was reached that the building should be available for a broad range of educational purposes, but the dean of education warned against "booking the center solidly and preventing the accommodation of University functions which, by their nature, cannot be planned for in advance."

Despite debate, maximum use of the facility continues to be a concern of the Continuing Education director. At the University of Oklahoma, normally empty times have been termed "disaster" periods. The "disaster" periods on weekends and from December 17 through the first week of January were estimated to account for about $41,000 diminished revenue during a year. In order to alleviate this "loss," the Continuing Education staff at a recent planning meeting decided that a bonus of 25% of the gross would be added to the budgets of the programmers who scheduled conferences during those periods. The idea was that this would provide more leeway for experimenting with programs that might not normally be expected to be self supporting. The staff also decided to urge "host conferences"—the non-staff developed kind of activity—to use "disaster" periods. In addition, the staff "brainstormed" to come up with new ideas to serve the double purpose of filling the empty rooms and providing experimental

Maximum use of his facility continues to be a concern of every Center director. "We want to keep the halls and the house full." Shown are corridors at the Oklahoma and Notre Dame Centers, *a* during a rush time and *b* during a slack period.

117

and educationally valid new programs. There was the idea of establishing "help" weekends for students of the correspondence study department. Another idea was the "weekend with a scholar," an inter-action group conference in which participants could explore a subject in depth with the guidance of a distinguished scholar. A third suggestion was a series of related weekend study seminars for individuals participating over several weekends.

All these were tried, and the results, according to one newspaper reporter, have provided a "welcome break from the humdrum routine of punching a time clock or washing dishes." Of the weekend seminars, she wrote:

*"Late on Friday afternoon they begin to check into rooms at Sooner House or the duplex cottages designed for families. Many arrive in time to have dinner at the Commons, where food service is supervised by Chef Thomas L. Farrell, one of the elite band of forty-seven North American chefs who have been awarded the Order of the Golden Torque.*

*"Relaxed and eager to get acquainted, the students meet in a conference room in the Forum building to hear faculty members and others present papers on the seminar topic, which might be religion, philosophy, drugs and society, the city, or poverty. This week it's history, and after the concluding talk by Dr. Arrell M. Gibson, OU faculty member whose books reflect his vast knowledge of Southwestern history, the fun begins. Everyone present has an opportunity to present his views and see how they match or conflict with those of people with different educations and experiences.*

*"'This is the first time in years I've had a chance to talk about anything but the weather, the crops, and the neighborhood news,' commented a rancher as a session ended one Saturday afternoon. 'You forget how really satisfying good conversation can be.'*

*"This fall the seminars will have a new format as the 'weekend university' is inaugurated. Fourteen programs will be offered on consecutive weekends by four departments of the College of Continuing Education—health studies, leadership training, liberal studies, and family life. A sample of the subjects includes 'Censorship: Art versus Obscenity,' 'Can You Afford Good Health?' 'Values in Conflict,' and 'Productive Thinking.' To date, about eighty percent of the people who have come to one seminar have returned for another.*

*"'This is vital business,' says Jerry Hargis, who arranges the weekend programs. 'We are helping adults cope intelligently with the problems of a constantly changing world. The day when an individual can consider his education complete has ended. Our very survival may depend on our willingness to continue to learn.'"*

## STAYING IN THE BLACK

Thus at Oklahoma the problem of "keeping the house full" led to successful innovative educational programming. But just getting people there for stimulating discussion was only part of it. Tending to their physical needs as temporary residents involved a large staff, careful planning, and good management. As a trade journal article, "A Hotel Is Not a Toy," pointed out: "A hotel manager should be many things. He must be a professional person and have good previous experience in his field. He should have a good formal education. He should be a good business manager and a good employer. Such managers are hard to find. Nevertheless, they are essential to the ultimate success of an operation of any significant size; responsibility for a one-million-dollar investment cannot be laid in the hands of a $7000-per-year man. It just does not work."

At Oklahoma, where the dean sought and got professional management for his facility operation, the financial records reflected professional guidance: income rose from $170,879 in 1962 to $333,085 in 1965; room occupancy increased during the same period from 46.6% to 52.6%; just between 1963 and 1964, the balance sheet changed from a loss of $32,572 to a profit of $12,598.

At Georgia, where the managerial services director is essentially an educator, having moved up through the programming staff, the business operation also prospered.

The Managerial Services Division has four departments:

1. The Business Affairs Department, in charge of budgeting, budget control, purchasing, receving of income, and expenditures for the total Continuing Education operation; nine full-time staff members are involved in the functions of the Business Affairs Department.

2. A Production Center which provides mailing and printing services for the Continuing Education program people; there are six full-time staff members and a number of part-time assistants, approximating two additional full-time people, who operate the Production Center.

3. The Plant Operations Service, involving sixteen individuals in building maintenance and grounds upkeep.

4. The Auxiliary Enterprises Department concerned with food, rooms, and gift shop operation.

The Foods Section of the Auxiliary Enterprises Department has forty-five full-time employees and fifty-five part-time. There is a food service director, three supervisors, two hostesses, two stock room attendants and thirty-eight kitchen employees; there are fifty-five part-time waiters and waitresses. The income from the food services is approximately $300,000 per year.

The Housing Service brings in about $265,000 a year, of which about 25% is used for non-housing expenses. The overall housing management involves one director, two supervisors and two secretaries. To operate the registration and information services there are four desk clerks, three switchboard

The main auditorium of the Georgia Center is patterned after the United Nations General Assembly room.

operators, and twenty part-time student bellboys. The room service staff consists of two housekeepers and twelve maids.

At Georgia there is also a gift shop for the convenience of guests, but the operation, employing one person, loses money.

Of the total income of the Georgia Continuing Education operation, only 22.2% was received from auxiliary enterprises in 1965–1966. Other sources of support were 26.3% from state allocations, 11.6% from federal grants and gifts, and 0.7% from overhead and miscellaneous. The two other divisions, Communications and Instructional Services, provided the rest of the income, 4.6% from Communications, and the largest single contribution, 34.6% from Instructional Services. The total expense for the Continuing Education Department was $2,379,000, leaving a net of $114,000.

The Georgia operation "stays in the black" and yet has an essential focus on program. The associate director for managerial services attributes this to six factors:

1. The Kellogg Foundation gave us enough money to develop a facility and, in addition, program support money for five years. This gave us a good beginning.

2. The ever-increasing number of individuals that participate in continuing education programs provides a broadening base of operations.

3. We have always been given fine support by the University administration and financial support from the State.

4. There is a cooperative attitude and a real desire to be of service on the total part of our staff.

120

5. Good management applies from the top down and the bottom up.

6. Financially we have always been in a position to experiment with new programs, some of which have been very successful while others have failed. Both eventualities have a place in a viable operation.

One of the real problems in financing a Center operation was recognized in a 1951 analysis at Michigan State before the first Kellogg Center opened. "Space allocations reveal that only 53.44% of the building is devoted to revenue producing space," a report stated. "In a typical hotel operation at least 90% of the space must be revenue producing." With non-revenue producing space a Center fact-of-life, staying in the black is a real and pressing problem to Center managers everywhere.

## REMODELING AND REPAIR

In addition, just as securing a foundation grant proved to be simply a first step in the building of the facility, completing the building and getting it into operation is also just a first step in the financial functioning of a Continuing Education Center and program. Remodeling and re-equipping is a continuous process. At Michigan State two major additions and countless minor alterations were necessary during the first decade of operation. At Georgia there was a slow but constant development of unfinished basement areas to serve as communications production rooms, and the need for additional dining facilities and more efficient kitchen arrangements culminated in a half million dollar addition, again within the first decade of operation.

In every center actual use patterns varied from those anticipated in planning. Oklahoma's octagonal conference rooms, ideal for discussion, were awkward for audio-visuals, and some rectangular rooms would be included in any expansion program. In 1963 Dean White of Oklahoma admitted, "We should have twice the number of bathrooms in the Hall of Advanced Study and we should have built a "State Room" for seated food service in the Commons." In a parenthesis White added, "Jake Neville (Michigan State) will say, 'I told you so'—he was right!"

Concern for cost and convenience is not restricted however, to deans and directors. At one Center, a frustrated housekeeper complained:

*"There are outside lights in the overhang above the top floor and in the lobby dome on the inside, for both of which there is no access. This means that in order to change fifty dollars worth of bulbs a thousand dollars will have to be spent to erect scaffolding.*

*"The pitch of the receiving ramp is so steep and unprotected that delivery trucks have great difficulty in getting out when snow is on the ground.*

*"Each bed is supplied with an expensive bedspread that can only be dry-cleaned. Curtains and drapes cost $30,000 and there is not a single spare to make rotation possible."*

None of these items is overwhelming in itself, but all are costly and annoying. As the writer of the trade journal article, "A Hotel Is Not a Toy," pointed out, an architect for a housing facility should be carefully chosen and should be experienced in hotel construction. "You," he wrote, "cannot afford to pay for the architect's education."

But even experienced architects sometimes fail to anticipate serious problems. At the Chicago Center the size and location of the freight elevator has been a constant sorrow. As one employee put it:

*"On the first floor, the elevator was built to open into a short hall that opens into the kitchen on one side and into the back of the cafeteria line on the other. Any tables or chairs needed for the first floor have to go through the area in which the kitchen crew is working in order to get to the door leading into the conference rooms. The linen room is in the basement as are the storage spaces for tables and chairs. All conference set-ups involving more or fewer chairs or tables require moves from basement storage. It is a real difficulty to get banquet tables into the small freight elevator, and anyhow the elevator is in almost constant use by the kitchen because foods storage, vegetable room, garbage room, coolers, and freezers are also all in the basement. Waiters carrying full trays and a pastry cook trying to work in the path of a houseman attempting to maneuver tables and truckloads of chairs present a situation full of interesting possibilities."*

Repair is a problem, too. Constant use erodes floors, furniture, fixtures and other facilities so that unless a systematic plan of renewal and repair is developed, a threadbare carpet, a broken chair, a dripping faucet or a lamp that doesn't light can change acceptance to annoyance and can inhibit rather than assist learning. In budgeting, therefore, some provision needs to be made for replacement and repair. At the University of Georgia, for example, 5% of the gross income from all sources is set aside for such deferred maintenance.

Then there is the constant pressure on personnel to get things in order. A supervisor reported:

*"Many times conferences are scheduled within the interval of an hour or so and require stripping a room set for, say, eighty people at tables set in classroom style to an informal setup having only a few chairs scattered about the room—or the reverse. Storage space being inadequate on the second floor, this means taking tables to the basement, and it often happens that I have to pull all the men from whatever they are doing to accomplish this. Conference*

*preparation involves checking all ash trays, cleaning all blackboards, dusting chairs, cleaning erasers, supplying and placing such things as paper, pencils, notebooks, podiums, ordering or removing trays, decanters, glasses, etc. Breaks require setting the room in order. When conferences do not break or end exactly on time, someone has to "hover." Eight hours of perpetual motion is required of housemen except for the two ten-minute breaks prescribed by the university."*

## PROGRAM BUDGETING

While room, board, maintenance, and operation constitute major preoccupations of business staffs at Continuing Education centers, program budgeting, involving an analysis of the cost of the program and the setting of participant fees, is of major concern to the conference coordinators. In an analysis prepared at the University of Chicago of reports from the several Continuing Education centers for conference programs held during 1966, it was found that fees ran from "no fee" to over $360 per conference participant. Thirty-eight percent of the fees were $5 per person or under, and 27% involved fees from $5 up to $20. A bare 10% of the fees were over $100. The same study indicated that approximately 59% of the fees charged were paid by individuals (although employers or others might reimburse them later), 19% were paid in a blanket sum by the conference sponsor, about 15% were financed by government grants, while only 5% were subsidized by university funds and 2% by private grants.

The basis for the fee charged is usually an estimate of the total conference expenses—consisting of the direct cost and a portion of the indirect cost

Registering for a conference at the Notre Dame Center.

involved in providing the Center's services—divided by the anticipated attendance. Each Center has its own method of estimating these costs, but perhaps the method used at Notre Dame is the most explicit and revealing.

The Notre Dame system of setting conference fees is based upon the recognition that the total activity operating expense is derived from: (a) an estimate of clerical and secretarial services necessary for all events; (b) the coordination and supervisory services necessary; (c) the general departmental expenses; and (d) the total specific activity expense.

The Notre Dame staff has developed a "unit costing system" for the services; that is, the staff had identified clerical and secretarial services that can be estimated in $20 units. For example, it has been estimated that envelope addressing costs about five cents per envelope, so one unit—$20— has been assigned for each 400 envelopes; the stuffing, sorting, stamping, and typing of items to be mailed has been assigned one unit for every 1500 items; the registration procedure has been assigned one unit for every fifty participants; and if proceedings and course materials are to be prepared, one unit is assigned for each ten pages. To determine the cost estimate for clerical and secretarial services, therefore, the total number of units is multiplied by $20.

Items of specific activity expense, which vary widely from conference to conference, involve amounts paid to lecturers, discussion leaders and other resource people for honoraria, travel expense, meals, and housing. All these items need to be estimated as specific activity expenses.

For the adult student participants there usually are luncheons, dinners, and refreshments which must be figured into the registration fee. Frequently, too, there will be busses and guides for tours, and notebooks, and other individual student supplies.

Audio-visual equipment use, telephone and telegraph expenses, perhaps flowers and decorations, and special photographs for publicity or for the files of the conference organization are additional specific activity expenses. At Notre Dame, where international conferences are often held, the cost of simultaneous translation services involving supervision, translators and equipment may be additional specific activity expenses.

A total figure can be arrived at for the clerical and secretarial services based on the unit system, and a total figure based on actual expenditures can be achieved for the specific activity expenses. However, two other categories of expenses, the coordination and supervisory services and general departmental expenses, must be added if a true cost figure for each conference is to be determined. Experience at Notre Dame has indicated that 50¢ per day per attendee is a workable estimate of coordination costs. A supervisory fee of $15 per work unit for the overseeing of the estimated clerical and secretarial services is added, and an overhead item based on 10% of the total specific activity expenses makes up the estimate for coordination and supervisory services. In addition, there is a general departmental expense item of $15 per work unit for supplies, equipment, and miscellaneous expenses.

The sum of these estimates provides the total cost of the conference, except that when an organization, which is essentially commercial in its orientation rather than educational, is assisted in developing a conference utilizing the Notre Dame Center for Continuing Education, an institutional charge is added.

The total expense either may be charged an organization in a lump sum or may be divided by the total expected registration to establish individual registrant fees. With expenses estimated carefully in this manner, the planning committee that has projected a program too expensive for the sponsoring organization, or amounting to too large an individual registration fee, can make adjustments in services used or in other items, in order to reduce the fee.

Although the unit estimate system used by Notre Dame is perhaps the most elaborate structure for estimating conference expenses and determining fees, all Center staffs use some form of experiential rules of thumb or budgeting guidelines. Nebraska, for instance, assesses a general fee of $2 for one day and $1 for each additional day to each participant in addition to specific estimated program costs. (Youth rates are one-half.) The general expectation is that each conference should pay for its own out-of-pocket

Busy lines at course registration desks, such as the one pictured at the Nebraska Center, help keep the Centers "in the black".

expenses and make a contribution to the supervisory and general departmental overhead.

For most of the courses planned at centers for Continuing Education, such "pricing" schedules and rules of thumb prove adequate. But for the innovator the necessity to stay in the black is sometimes very constraining. For example, Dean Sol Tax at the University of Chicago wrote to the Kellogg Foundation seeking additional financial assistance for his plan to develop conference models such as the "Draft Conference" and the "Origins of Man," which had received creativity awards from the National University Extension Association. Tax said:

*"Although the conferences developed in terms of these models have proved significant, further development of experimental models in uniquely important conferences is contingent upon the establishment of certain rather than speculative financial bases for programming. The current practice of funding conferences on an ad hoc basis has tended to discourage faculty participation, has complicated the planning process, has been costly in terms of staff time, and has, at times, caused the abandonment of promising programs . . . . The problem is simply that the Center cannot request funds for a major conference before inviting scholars to participate in the conference; at the same time, the Center cannot invite scholars to participate in the conference before funds for the conference are committed."*


COOPERATION IS THE KEY

But whether financing is eventually made more and more a planned part of the total university commitment or whether it continues to remain essentially "speculative" and self-supporting, the undertaking of the Continuing Education enterprise remains complex and challenging. The lesson to be learned from an analysis of a variety of operations and organizational patterns is that President Coffman's original dictum was a wise one: a single director and/or a clear line of responsibility which focuses all phases of the operation on program development and support is essential. The key is cooperation: the housekeeping staff, the registration people, the food manager, the parking attendant, the accountant, and all other personnel are there to make effective education possible; the janitor must be concerned that the room is set up properly for the meeting even though last minute changes may be involved; the balance sheet must be subordinate to the program evaluation questionnaire even though some of the figures thereby turn out to be red. Nonetheless, the program staff has an equal and opposite responsibility if it is to continue to exist: program directors, coordinators, and planners must be concerned that financing is sufficient to support the edu-

# UNIVERSITY OF OKLAHOMA

## FIVE YEAR ANALYSIS OF SALARIES, WAGES AND FEES IN TERMS OF PERCENTAGE INCREASE OVER BASE YEAR 1962–63, ($1,303,000.00)

Payroll expenditures for The College of Continuing Education and The Division of Extension and Public Service including budgets, auxiliary enterprises, grants, and contracts during the period of 1962–63 to 1966–67

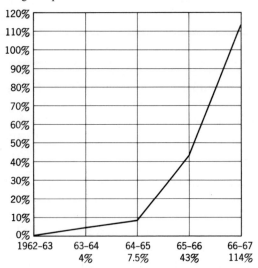

| | 1962-63 | 63-64 | 64-65 | 65-66 | 66-67 |
|---|---|---|---|---|---|
| | | 4% | 7.5% | 43% | 114% |

## OKLAHOMA CENTER FOR CONTINUING EDUCATION

% CONFERENCE ROOM OCCUPANCY FISCAL YEARS
ENDING JUNE 30TH, 1964, 1965, 1966, 1967

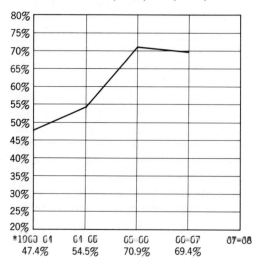

| *1963-64 | 64-65 | 65-66 | 66-67 | 67-68 |
|---|---|---|---|---|
| 47.4% | 54.5% | 70.9% | 69.4% | |

127

cational activity; each expenditure planned and made must contribute to educational effectiveness; planning and communications procedures need to be devised so that neither money nor staff time is wasted. The effective financial operation of a Continuing Education enterprise is one in which all efforts are designed to support the educational process, but one in which the educational process is so valuable that everyone—participants, parent institution, and public and private agencies outside the institution—is willing to support it.

## SEVERAL SOURCES FOR CENTER SUPPORT

Throughout this book, emphasis has been on the Continuing Education centers supported by initial contributions from the Kellogg Foundation. These, however, constitute only a small percentage of the total number of Continuing Education Centers in educational institutions in the United States. In addition, private industry and such other organizations as churches and labor groups have developed and are operating continuing education centers.

Among other sources of support are federal agencies. The Minnesota Center, first of the specially designed campus facilities, was funded by the Federal Public Works Agency, a depression-born source of funding which no longer exists; new federal legislation, however, may well provide funding in the late sixties and the seventies.

In June 1967 a sum of $371,685 was granted to the New England Center for Continuing Education for the construction of educational facilities included in first phase construction. The grant was made under Title I of the Higher Education Facilities Act by the United States Department of Health, Education, and Welfare.

The Center has additional eligibility and a request will be made soon for a second federal grant to be applied to first-phase construction. Eligibility applies to the learning center portion of the complex only; the high rise towers to be used for sleeping quarters are not included.

Another source of support for educational agencies wishing to develop Continuing Education Centers is the private philanthropy embodied in the transfer of existing properties from private to educational purposes. Such was the source of the University of Illinois' Allerton House and Syracuse University's Pinebrook Center, both of which were established in the late nineteen forties as a result of the gift of a magnificent mansion on spacious grounds to the University of Illinois and a fifty-four acre lake resort in the Adirondack mountains to Syracuse.

Washington University of St. Louis took a similar gift of property in the Ozarks and was able, through contributions of funds by business and indus-

trial organizations, to construct a group of buildings designated the Brom-woods Center; none of the individual gifts was large, but each contributed to the building of a specific unit of the Center. Expansion of the facility is continuing through similar gifts applied to developing needs.

A financial fact-of-life for a Continuing Education Center is that substantial amounts of money are needed both for construction and maintenance of such a facility. The operation of the food and housing enterprises requires large specialized staffs. Effective programs involve the employment of capable managers and coordinators as well as the participation of lecturers and discussion leaders who frequently command impressive fees. Expense to the individual participant involves, in addition to the program fees themselves, time away from the job as well as travel, meals, and lodging. As a result, the building and operation of a Continuing Education Center demands a substantial institutional commitment both educationally and financially; it involves the solicitation of outside funds either through philanthropy of government support; it frequently necessitates a mortgage obligation or bond issues; it always calls for continuing maintenance and anticipation of expansion and remodeling. Financial stress and strain continue throughout the existence of a Continuing Education Center. The development of the educational program also involves institutional and outside support, while most adult student participation derives from some form of expense-account financing.

But all these sources exist and contribute. Contemporary Continuing Education fits the needs of mid-Twentieth Century Society: it provides knowledge necessary for survival and provides it at a time, at a place and in a manner appropriate to the work and life patterns of today. Because of its appropriateness and effectiveness, Continuing Education is prospering both financially and educationally.

## LISTING OF U.S. RESIDENTIAL CENTERS
## FOR CONTINUING EDUCATION*

| NAME OF RESIDENTIAL FACILITY | LOCATION | DATE OF ESTABLISHMENT |
|---|---|---|
| Dorothy Hall Guest House, Tuskegee Institute | Tuskegee Institute, Alabama | |
| Educational Center, California State Polytechnic College, Kellogg-Voorhis Unit | Pomona, California | 1961 |
| The University of California Residential Conference Center | Lake Arrowhead, California | 1957 |

| | | |
|---|---|---|
| University of Southern California Conference Center | Idyllwild, California | 1962 |
| Bay Campus, University of South Florida | St. Petersburg, Florida | 1963 |
| Chinsegut Hill Continuing Education Center, University of South Florida | Tampa, Florida | 1965 |
| Georgia Center for Continuing Education, University of Georgia | Athens, Georgia | 1957 |
| East-West Center | Honolulu, Hawaii | 1960 |
| Allerton House, University of Illinois | Monticello, Illinois | 1949 |
| Hott Memorial Center, University of Illinois | Monticello, Illinois | 1962 |
| University Center, Northern Illinois University | DeKalb, Illinois | 1966 |
| The University of Chicago Center for Continuing Education, | Chicago, Illinois | 1963 |
| Biddle Continuation Center, Indiana University | Bloomington, Indiana | 1959 |
| Bradford Woods, Indiana University | Martinsville, Indiana | 1953 |
| Center for Continuing Education University of Notre Dame | Notre Dame, Indiana | 1966 |
| Kitselman Conference Center, Ball State University | Muncie, Indiana | 1957 |
| Memorial Center, Purdue University | Lafayette, Indiana | 1958 |
| Iowa Center for Continuation Study, University of Iowa | Iowa City, Iowa | 1952 |
| Washburn University Adult Education Center | Topeka, Kansas | |
| Carnahan House Conference Center, University of Kentucky | Lexington, Kentucky | 1962 |
| Pleasant Hall, The Louisiana State University Adult Education Center | Baton Rouge, Louisiana | 1954 |
| Center of Adult Education, University of Maryland | College Park, Maryland | 1964 |
| Donaldson Brown Center, University of Maryland | Port Deposit, Maryland | 1966 |
| Endicott House, Massachusetts Institute of Technology | Dedham, Massachusetts | 1955 |
| Henderson House, Northeastern University | Weston, Massachusetts | 1961 |
| Osgood Hill, Boston University Conference Center | North Andover, Massachusetts | |

130

| | | |
|---|---|---|
| Themis House Conference Center, Brandeis University | Waltham, Massachusetts | 1962 |
| Bellemont Manor, Continuing Education Center, Albion College | Albion, Michigan | 1963 |
| Don H. Bottum University Center, Northern Michigan University | Marquette, Michigan | 1960 |
| Dow Leadership Conference Center, Hillsdale College | Hillsdale, Michigan | 1965 |
| Fairlane Mansion, Dearborn Campus, University of Michigan | Dearborn, Michigan | |
| Gull Lake Center for Continuing Education, Michigan State University | Hickory Corners, Michigan | 1954 |
| Kellogg Center for Continuing Education, Michigan State University | East Lansing, Michigan | 1951 |
| McGregor Memorial Conference Center, Wayne State University | Detroit, Michigan | |
| Michigan Tech Conference Center, Michigan Technological University | Houghton, Michigan | 1956 |
| University of Minnesota Center for Continuation Study | Minneapolis, Minnesota | 1936 |
| Mississippi Center for Continuation Study, University of Mississippi | University, Mississippi | 1954 |
| Bromwoods, Washington University Conference Center | Grubville, Missouri | 1961 |
| Fordyce House, Saint Louis University | St. Louis, Missouri | 1967 |
| University of Nebraska Center for Continuing Education | Lincoln, Nebraska | 1961 |
| Center for Continuing Education, University of Nevada | Reno, Nevada | 1967 |
| New England Center for Continuing Education, University of New Hampshire | Durham, New Hampshire | 1966 |
| Newark College of Engineering Continuing Education Center | Newark, New Jersey | 1966 |
| The Lawrence Ranch, The University of New Mexico | Albuquerque, New Mexico | 1963 |
| Arden House, Graduate School of Business, Columbia University | Harriman, New York | 1950 |
| International Center for Continuing Education, Columbia University | New York, New York | 1966 |
| Camp Arnot, Cornell University | Ithaca, New York | |

| | | |
|---|---|---|
| Continuing Education Center,<br>for the Public Service,<br>Syracuse University | Syracuse, New York | |
| The Graduate Center,<br>Polytechnic Institute of<br>Brooklyn | Farmingdale, L.I.,<br>New York | 1961 |
| Greyston Conference Center,<br>Teachers College,<br>Columbia University | New York, New York | 1963 |
| Institute for Community Education,<br>Hofstra University | Hempstead, New York | 1966 |
| The International Center,<br>State University of New York | Oyster Bay, L.I.,<br>New York | |
| Minnowbrook Conference Center of<br>Syracuse University | Blue Mountain Lake,<br>New York | 1954 |
| Pinebrook Conference Center of<br>Syracuse University | Upper Saranac Lake,<br>New York | 1948 |
| Sagamore Conference Center of<br>Syracuse University | Raquette Lake,<br>New York | 1954 |
| Syracuse University Center | Syracuse, New York | |
| Quail Roost Conference Center,<br>University of North Carolina | Rougemont,<br>North Carolina | 1965 |
| Alexander House,<br>Antioch College | Yellow Springs, Ohio | 1963 |
| Bergamo,<br>University of Dayton, East Campus | Dayton, Ohio | 1967 |
| Institute for Civic Education,<br>University of Ohio | Akron, Ohio | 1956 |
| Public Affairs Conference Center,<br>Kenyon College | Gambier, Ohio | 1966 |
| Oklahoma Center for Continuing<br>Education,<br>University of Oklahoma | Norman, Oklahoma | 1962 |
| Student Union,<br>Oklahoma State University | Stillwater, Oklahoma | |
| J. Orvis Keller Bldg.,<br>Conference Center,<br>Pennsylvania State University | University Park,<br>Pennsylvania | |
| Continuing Education Center,<br>Southern Methodist University | Dallas, Texas | 1965 |
| The Adult Education Center,<br>Goddard College | Plainfield, Vermont | 1963 |
| Airlie Foundation Center,<br>George Washington University | Warrenton, Virginia | 1961 |
| Donaldson Brown Continuing<br>Education Center,<br>Virginia Polytechnic Institute | Blacksburg, Virginia | 1968 |
| Virginia State College Residential<br>Facility | Petersburg, Virginia | 1947 |

132

| | | |
|---|---|---|
| Continuing Education Center, University of Washington | Lake Wilderness, Washington | 1967 |
| Jackson's Mill, West Virginia University | Weston, West Virginia | 1922 |
| Mont Chateau Lodge, West Virginia University | Cheat Lake, West Virginia | 1967 |
| Towers Conference Center, West Virginia University | Morgantown, West Virginia | 1966 |
| Carthage College Continuing Education Center | Kenosha, Wisconsin | 1965 |
| Lake Geneva Campus, George Williams College | Williams Bay, Wisconsin | 1884 |
| Kenwood Conference Center, University of Wisconsin-Milwaukee | Milwaukee, Wisconsin | |
| The Wisconsin Center, University of Wisconsin | Madison, Wisconsin | 1958 |
| Schwinn-University of Wyoming Conference Center | Dubois, Wyoming | 1963 |
| Trail Lake Ranch Conference Center, University of Wyoming | Dubois, Wyoming | 1960 |

* List provided by the Continuing Education Studies and Training Program, The Department of Education, University of Chicago, and restricted to Continuing Education Centers owned by or affiliated with universities and colleges.

CHAPTER 7

# Where Do We Go from Here?
# Continuing Education Centers
# Today and Tomorrow

In 1951 the first Kellogg Foundation-assisted Center for Continuing Education at Michigan State University was opened. In 1968 construction on the last two Kellogg-assisted Centers for Continuing Education at the University of New Hampshire and at Columbia University was in progress. In 1951 there were just five university-based Centers for Continuing Education in operation, and by 1968 there were approximately 80 such centers. During the intervening years, the Kellogg Foundation invested more than $20,000,000 to assist Continuing Education Programs in the building of facilities and in initial operations. At a meeting in the Chicago Center, it asked leaders in the Continuing Education movement to reflect on the years since 1951 and to suggest what, if anything, had been accomplished.

"First of all," Professor Cyril O. Houle, of the University of Chicago, said, "I think the fact that there are now about 80 residential centers is very important and illustrates that the ideas supported by the Foundation have been accepted. The development of these centers has clearly been stimulated by the examples of the Kellogg Centers. The Foundation spent about $20,000,000 but the total expenditures might very accurately be estimated at from 100 to 125 million."

Emory W. Morris, head of the Kellogg Foundation, agreed. "Now we're receiving inquiries from all over the world about Continuing Education," he said. "You pioneers have created a problem for us through your accomplishment. We don't have the money to replicate Continuing Education Centers around the globe but we do have an obligation to try to establish guidelines that would be helpful to people who want to replicate them."

"We'll have to remember," Professor Houle pointed out, "that, in one sense Continuing Education applies to virtually the whole range of adult education. In another sense it has been used to refer more specifically to the

134

Cyril O. Houle

residential conferences carried on in the Kellogg-assisted Centers. Probably in our discussion, we shouldn't undertake to deal with all the problems of society or of adult education in general, but we can take a good hard look at the residential centers."

"Of course we can," Thurman White, Dean of Continuing Education at the University of Oklahoma, said. "We've been involved in University residential Continuing Education for quite awhile. We know some things. We've learned some lessons. We can put our experiences in the pot and talk about what we've tried and what, to date has been most useful."

## FOUNDATION-AIDED
## CONTINUING EDUCATION CENTERS

| Sponsoring University | Year Established | Foundation Grants |
|---|---|---|
| Michigan State University | 1951 | $ 2,124,479 |
| University of Georgia | 1957 | 2,444,000 |
| University of Nebraska | 1961 | 1,856,000 |
| University of Oklahoma | 1962 | 1,845,000 |
| University of Chicago | 1963 | 3,182,573 |
| University of Notre Dame | 1965 | 1,543,400 |
| Oxford University (England) | 1965 | 135,100 |
| New England Center (at University of New Hampshire) | 1965*/1966* | 2,419,000 |
| Columbia University | 1966* | 1,511,573 |
| California Polytechnic State College | 1968* | 3,000,000 |
| | TOTAL | $20,061,125 |

* Year of grant. Center currently under construction.

Sol Tax           Thurman White

Also, what have been our failures," interjected Sol Tax, Dean of Extension at the University of Chicago. "We need to see if we have learned anything from our mistakes as well as from our successes."

## NUMBERS OF CONFERENCES INCREASE

"In the case of our Center," H. R. Neville, Provost at Michigan State University, said, "our first year of operation saw almost a 115% increase

Emory W. Morris

H. R. Neville

in the number of conferences offered at the University and, while most conferences were offered for smaller groups than in the past, there was more than a 75% increase in the number of people who attended."

"We had the same experience at Georgia," Dr. Hugh Masters, Director of Continuing Education at the University of Georgia, said. " In our first year there was a 92% increase in the number of conferences and more than a 76% increase in the number of registrations."

Dr. White nodded. "Not only that," he said, "but the Oklahoma Center has become an enormous stimulant to the development of new programs

Hugh Masters

137

of Continuing Education on the University of Oklahoma campus. It has brought us grants in Liberal Education, Urban Science, Human Relations, Industrial Development, and appropriations for law enforcement education and health studies. The fact of a curriculum for an adult student body is slowly being established. Its parts are still so discrete that it may not attract a person annually for all his adult years, but it can for at least ten years involve a great many individuals."

"Right from the start," Dr. Neville pointed out, "the Continuing Education Service housed in the Kellogg Center included university extension classes, correspondence study, community service, telecourses, speakers bureau, and the administration of regional offices in addition to the conference and institute programs. The existence of the Center," he said, "has focused attention on the whole range of Continuing Education activities."

"Not only that," Masters added, "the Centers have had a special impact on off-campus agencies. Many groups within the general public are beginning to think in terms of Continuing Education—corporations, for example."

"Yes," Neville agreed, "it may very well be that the Kellogg Foundation has fostered an idea which has now been picked up by all of society. Pre-war hotels did not cater to educational groups nor to conference groups. My guess is that every hotel that is built now is designed with the notion in mind that meetings of all kinds would be held there; and, in large part, these are educational meetings. It may be that in our time Continuing Education of professionals and all kinds of people is so important that not only do universities involve themselves in this work, but also hotel corporations."

## UNIVERSITY RESOURCES IMPORTANT

Dr. Morris nodded. "The Foundation, however," he said, "has aided only those programs that were in the context of a great university with vast intellectual resources and service—and not, as with some of the requests that we received, under the umbrella of institutions with few resources where there would perhaps be more harm done than good. It seems to me that Continuing Education must be buttressed by many resources."

"All right," someone said, "but even if we agree that Continuing Education needs the intellectual resources and orientation of a university or at least of an organization that is essentially educative, haven't we forgotten the word 'residential' in our discussion of 'residential Continuing Education?' We say the Center generates more conferences and more people attend. We say it focuses attention on old programs and brings new ones. We say it even gets new agencies into the business. So what? Bigness and busyness aren't necessarily good. Isn't it important to involve the 'whole man' and provide a 'total experience,' preferably by gathering a small group in a rural setting somewhat reminiscent of the Danish Folk High School? There aren't any 'true' residential values in the 'typical' procedure at one of your huge, hotel-like structures—no values like withdrawal from normal environment for a period of continuous, interpersonal involvement and a deep, intense feeling of participation through a penetrating immersion in the subject matter."

Robert Schact of the University of Wisconsin was cited as characterizing the "tailor-made, package programs" in this way:

*"Someone in some office has planned the program, signed a sheaf of appoint-ment forms for the experts who are to speak, and turned the details over to the 'conference office.'*

*"The participants arrive, check into their comfortable rooms equipped with running ice water, radio, television, and air conditioning; go through the standard registration procedure; and for the next several days are part of a large audience—or at best, somewhat involved participants in a combination of general sessions, smaller work groups, banquets, and late evening gatherings in the larger suites of the more hospitable members."*

"Many people will argue that a properly designed conference in a large Center can have those 'residential values,'" Professor Houle said. "Certainly there's an emotional tension that envelops both staff and students as the conference cycle runs its course."

"Everything depends on effective resource utilization," Arthur Adams, of the University of New Hampshire said. "I recall reading somewhere that the Chicago Center was dubbed the 'Egghead Hotel' in a newspaper item when it was being built, and I think that's not such a terrible thing. Certainly, the importance of Continuing Education has been recognized by the hotel and resort industry. Scarcely a day passes when I do not receive an advertise-ment from some such establishment which points out, in beautifully colored lithographs, the attractive features of the place and the recreational delights that it offers. Such brochures do not speak, however, of what to me is an essential factor, one which is missing in the hotel and resort conference center. This essential feature is educational direction and support. If Continuing Education is to be truly meaningful, it requires thoughtful involvement in the planning, in relating the facilities to the offerings, and in providing reference resources of pertinent significance."

## CONTINUING EDUCATION APPROPRIATE FOR UNIVERSITY

"Perhaps we can't resolve some of the basic philosophical issues here and now," Provost Neville said. "However, as a practical matter, before the Centers came into existence, conference activities on most campuses sprouted

Arthur Adams

wherever some faculty member had a particular interest, and they grew like weeds, in a disorderly and confused way. The Centers have served as a focal point on those campuses, and the faculty has begun to look to the Center for direction and leadership in Continuing Education activities. I think one of the greatest strengths the Kellogg Foundation has given by providing Centers on campuses is that the Centers have clearly identified Continuing Education as an appropriate function for universities and have cast it in the best light."

"I agree," said Dean Andrew Cordier of Columbia University. "As our new Center for Continuing Education at the School of International Affairs nears completion, we're involved in activities of greater scope and depth than ever before in our history. At least twelve groups are now engaged in extensive planning for at least as many conferences, all of very prestigious and timely character."

## GROUPS RETURN FOR "CONTINUING STUDY"

"You can look at the numbers another way," said Dr. Masters. "If groups and individuals come to the Center just once for a one- or two-day session,

140

the educational impact may be very slight. But if the same groups return year-after-year for 'continuing' study there is the likelihood that the experience will be more rewarding. At Georgia we were pleased to see that during the second year of the Center's operation 60% of the conferences involved groups who had attended the first year."

"We think sequence offerings are particularly important," said Dean White of the University of Oklahoma. "We're proud that nearly 40% of our conferences are specifically designed to be of a continuing nature and we're working to develop a truly 'continuing' adult student body."

"At Georgia we have created one- two- and three-year sequence classes," Dr. Masters said. "We award a certificate on the completion of the total program. Another thing we like to see is growing participation by our faculty. In our first year, for instance, 171 faculty members took part in conferences; by 1963 this had increased to 227."

"And every college or division in the University has sponsored some conferences at the Nebraska Center," said Dean Janike of the University of Nebraska. "Of course, Agriculture and Home Economics is the big user, but the College of Arts and Sciences sponsors almost as many sessions as does Business."

"So you've got lots of people coming back year after year, and the faculty are finding their way in through the front door," said the objector. "But

Andrew Cordier

Jess Burkett

what's new about all this? You all agree these things were going on before the Centers were built. Just more of the same doesn't sound like much progress."

## NEW PROGRAMS DEVELOPED

"It's pretty hard to argue that our Bachelor of Liberal Studies degree is 'old hat,' " Dr. Jess Burkett, Assistant Dean at the University of Oklahoma pointed out. "This was a program devised by a faculty study committee and involved both independent study and residential experiences at the Center over a period of several years in a pattern that is totally new to higher education in the United States, and it leads to a totally new degree at the University of Oklahoma. Now a Master of Liberal Studies degree has been approved. A graduate degree by independent study is certainly new."

"And don't forget our advanced program in government," Dean White nudged. "It's a graduate program, too, one that combines independent reading and research problems with a series of one-week, five-hour-per-day, intensive resident study sessions at the Center."

"Certainly, without the electronic facilities for simultaneous translation, without closed circuit television, and without functionally designed small conference rooms in close conjunction with our auditorium, we could not have held our multilingual Vatican II discussion," added Dean Thomas Bergin of Notre Dame.

"We've tried some new things, too," Dean Janike said, "and maybe it points up one value of a Center for Continuing Education to admit that in our Hall of Youth at Nebraska we have had some rather spectacular failures as well as successes. We started off bravely with what we called the Midwest Institute for Young Adults, one part of which was an eight-week session in agricultural topics and the other was a similar eight-week session in business topics, chosen to assist rural youth in the transition from a farm to urban economy. The first year only 50 students enrolled, three-fourths of them for agriculture.

142

E. W. Janike

"Chancellor Hardin then appointed a carefully selected group of faculty and Nebraska businessmen to develop the business side of the program. The next year a business course, specifically designed to develop a knowledge of the farm implement field, yielded virtually no registrations despite intensive promotion through approximately twelve hundred member firms of the Midwest Retail Farm Equipment Association. Even in agriculture,

Thomas Bergin

143

the eight-week term appeared too long, and when the opening date of the course in the fall term conflicted with corn picking operations, only 14 students attended. The next year, the business course was dropped completely and the starting date for the agriculture short course was set back until December. The result was that 59 students enrolled.

"The failure of the business course was a disappointment, but even more disappointing was a remedial course established for freshmen who were having academic difficulty. Twenty-one students enrolled on the assurance that satisfactory completion of the short course would entitle them to re-admission to the University. Sixteen did return, but their record after the second semester was: none in good standing, three on probation, and thirteen suspended. We've tried new things all right, and the fact that some haven't worked won't keep us from trying more."

"The kind of thing we're attempting is new, too," said Dr. Harry P. Day, Director of the New England Center. "Cooperation between six State Universities, making mutual financial contributions to a joint regional continuing education effort is something that has never been attempted before. And if it works in Continuing Education there is every reason to believe that cooperation can be extended into other areas of mutual concern."

"We developed a cooperative relationship with the State Department of Public Instruction to combine our television facilities so that day and evening educational television would reach approximately eighty percent of the people

Harry P. Day

of Georgia," Dr. Masters said. "The potential impact on both children and adults is enormous. We were awarded the 1967 national Distinguished Achievement Award by the American Association of Colleges for Teacher Education for our network program beamed four times a week to 900 elementary school mathematics teachers in 35 state viewing centers."

"Yes, some of you are plowing new ground," the doubter agreed. "But you really haven't come to grips with my first question yet. How do you know that what you are doing is accomplishing its goals? Except for the failures at Nebraska none of you has indicated any actual efforts at program evaluation."

## EVALUATION IS A REAL NEED

"Evaluation is a real need," Provost Neville said.

"But we do have a joint-reporting process under way," Professor Houle pointed out.

Provost Neville nodded. "We've been working on ways of evaluating conferences and sharing information for a long time," he said. "Remember, back in 1959 we had a conference for the Kellogg-assisted Center people, and about 20 program coordinators and directors showed up. We had a three-day meeting, exploring and exchanging ideas on Continuing Education. I recall that even then our big concern was to figure out how best to integrate and coordinate the educational services with the physical plant operation and food and housing."

## DATA COLLECTING DEVELOPED

"It wasn't until 1962, though, that we really began to get down to work," Dean White said. "There was a meeting at the Nebraska Center and before we broke up we appointed a committee to begin work on a data-collection instrument. I remember that clearly because the committee had its first meeting next at the University of Oklahoma."

"We put one of our interns on it," Professor Houle said, "and he worked with a sub-committee to draft a questionnaire that he went over at a meeting in December 1963, at the Chicago Center."

There was a trial run in January 1964. Then there was another six-month trial run. In 1965 the committee voted to do a full year's collection and to invite the University of Illinois, Syracuse University, Washington University at St. Louis, Wayne State University, and the University of Minnesota to join in. By the summer of 1966, there was sufficient information for a preliminary report but it was obvious that the format was clumsy and a new format was decided on.

"Now I guess we're all set for continuing the study for several years," Professor Houle said. "Thanks to the Kellogg Foundation, we have some personnel to organize the data, we can afford some computer time for analysis, and then there is money for printing and some travel funds."

"Yes," the doubter agreed, "you're adding all your numbers together now and coming up with some pretty big totals. But what about real research? What about some solid empirical studies that get at the effectiveness of what you're doing?"

## RESEARCH STUDIES UNDERWAY

"We started our research program a year before the Center was built," Dean Janike said. "Alan Knox was hired as director of research and he set out on two major studies, one he called the base-line study of adult participation in Nebraska, involving interviews with 1500 adults representing the total adult population between 21 and 69 years of age. He did a broadside study of adult learning, too; that was a cooperative project with six other universities in which he was trying to get at the variables that had the most influence on achievement and withdrawal of adults who were participating in educational programs."

"In our Studies and Training Program at the University of Chicago," Professor Houle said, "graduate students are developing substantial studies that range all the way from the history of residential adult education to basic research in adult learning."

"There have been other studies, too," Provost Neville said. "There was a 1961 study called 'A Comparison of the Effectiveness of Adult Residential and Non-residential Learning Situations,' in which two groups studied the same material presented by the same teachers, one group working in a regular spaced-learning class situation and the other group participating in a concentrated residential study program. The results showed that although there were no significant differences in the amount of tested knowledge gained, the residential group had positive changes of attitude that didn't occur in the non-residential group."

"Research was an integral part of our Oklahoma proposal to the Foundation," Dean White said, "but I'm sorry to report that we have really done very little with it. We clearly need at least one full-time research mind at work."

"There is no doubt that we're delinquent in the matters of evaluation and research," Dr. Masters said. "But it is obvious that more and more studies are being undertaken."

"And with the increasing number of practitioners who have now had graduate training in the field of adult education," Professor Houle said, "the need for substantial studies will be matched by the availability of people capable of performing the rigorous scholarly tasks involved."

"But where will it all lead?" the doubter asked. "If all you're going to do is more and more of the same kind of thing, a few studies here and there aren't going to amount to much."

## MORE EMPHASIS IN FUTURE

"Even if that were all we were doing," Provost Neville said, "it would be worth while. The fact is that in the years ahead there is going to be more emphasis on Continuing Education rather than less."

"There is no doubt about it," said Dr. Masters, "and we're going to have to extend ourselves in two directions at once. First of all, people nowadays —and even more in the future—have to participate in actions over which they have no control. The interdependence of human beings is such that at the most we can influence directly only the immediate situation in which we find ourselves. In order to do our jobs and in order to understand the complex situation in which we find ourselves, we're going to have to learn, then learn again, then learn again and again and again. And in order to be of real influence, Continuing Education is going to have to concentrate on individuals who are in policy-making positions whether at the local level or in international affairs. At the same time, though, we're going to have to reach more low-income groups—President Hannah and I both used the term 'little guy' to designate the kind of person who should benefit from the Center when we were evaluating on the original Michigan State proposal. We're going to have to broaden our concept of University education to include not only sophisticated intellectual subject matter but also the total life of the individual, including his family relationships and his recreational patterns. We're going to need to make knowledge as available as running water. We're going to have to concentrate on educational activities that have leading-on values or characteristics: an educational experience at the Center should lead the participants on into related and continuing activities in his life outside the Center."

"Let me tell you about Chicago's newest and most exciting program," Dean Sol Tax said. "We call it a 'Community Service Workshop,' and it was funded through Title I of the Higher Education Act of 1965.

"The thing that started it was the requirement in the Economic Opportunity Act that there should be 'maximum participation in the solution of community problems by indigenous members of the communities.' Now that's easy to say, but it's hard to do because indigenous members of the community frequently have no background or perspective for planning or carrying out development projects. So we set up a year-long program to involve some 100 people—a really heterogenous group of indigenous community leaders, educators, and administrators and line staff from public and private agencies—in a series of residential seminars where they could, first of all, simply get acquainted and then get on with the business of building up a background of theoretical understanding and a study of real-life models of successful indigenous community developments.

"We had three phases. First there was a five-day seminar in October for general orientation dealing with the concepts of power and responsibility, social service and social change, and the development of grass roots leadership. Our basic theme was, 'Whose sores of discontent get rubbed raw for whose benefit?' Then there were three weekend seminars—one in January, one in February, and one in March—to look intensively and specifically at welfare, education and urban renewal. Finally there were three concluding seminars clustered in the last week of May and the first two weeks of June to grapple with youth problems, view successful action models, and come to grips with local planning.

"We made the seminars residential to get people from the whole region together and away from the day-to-day pressures of their environment and jobs, to give plenty of time in the evening and at meal breaks for informal discussion, and to provide continuity and concentration for study in depth. Most seminars were on weekends since the participants were employed full-time elsewhere. Team teaching—the use of five or six action and research groups for instruction and discussion leadership—gave a chance for total participation and mutual sharing of knowledge and experience. The workshop members themselves shaped the design and content of the successive seminars.

"Exchanges between participants were illuminating and sometimes brutally frank. The confrontation between representatives of realtor boards and tenant unions involved both heat and light, the latter largely because the residential situation of the workshop necessitated continuing contact and discussion beyond cliche and on toward truth. A representative of the Chicago Board of Health effected immediate changes in policy and operation as a result of his involvement in the workshop.

"We had resource people here from Washington, D.C., Jackson, Mississippi, Berkeley, San Francisco, Harlem, and St. Louis. All expenses of workshop participants and resource people were paid from the start so that no one had to be left out because he couldn't afford to come.

"Now that it's over, participants are continuing to meet regularly on their own in downtown locations and are planning non-residential extensions of the seminars into neighborhoods and out-state communities. I don't know at this point what the range and depth of the effect of their workshop will be, but the training and involvement of indigenous community leaders in policy decisions as well as action programs affecting their own destiny is certain to have profound influence on the future. We think this is an innovative Continuing Education program if there ever was one."

Mrs. Lucy Ann Marx, Director of the Chicago Center for Continuing Education, was in agreement with Dean Tax, and added:

"Continuing Education also has a role in contributing to the knowledge explosion by developing conferences during which attempts would be made to identify and integrate existing knowledge and to establish directions for continued research in the various academic disciplines. The purposes of such conferences would be to contribute to and evaluate current knowledge. Given the positions of Centers within university communities, it seems to me that Centers for Continuing Education have a unique opportunity to make this sort of contribution."

Arthur Adams of the University of New Hampshire nodded. "I am persuaded," he said, "that Continuing Education is likely to become one of the major segments of our total national educational effort. I am impressed by the fact that I have, during the last year, engaged in a number of long conversations about the way in which an individual can become fully competent professionally and, at the same time, have a sufficiently wide range of interests to be able to adapt to the rapid changes which our society is experiencing. We all recognize that times are changing fast, but like the

Lucy Ann Marx

queen in *Alice in Wonderland,* we run fast to stay in the same place. Continuing Education offers the opportunity to project our thoughts toward the possibilities of the future and I submit that only those who can so project their thoughts are likely to find themselves in tune with the society and the economy we are likely to have in the days ahead.

"As any author knows, the most difficult part of writing is not what to put in, but what to leave out. I think the same thing is true of our response to the so-called explosion of knowledge. In our formal educational processes, we try to take account of new developments in every field, but we do not reorganize knowledge so as to put it into useful perspective for the future. Such reorganization would require leaving out those items of knowledge which have become obsolescent, but this is difficult to do, for there are many stout defenders of the status quo among our faculties. Continuing Education suffers no such limitations of form and tradition. It is free to deal with the new and to discard the obsolete, with the result that it can offer suggested possibilities for the future."

"The really new trend that we've observed at Michigan State," said Provost Neville, "is the long-term residential seminar—the one lasting from three weeks to six months—and our facilities just don't work out for those seminars."

Armand Hunter, Michigan State Director of Continuing Education, agreed. "Our twin-bed rooms, with one study table, closet, and bath, are fine for the purpose for which they were designed—the two- or three-day

Armand Hunter

conference," he said. "But strangers don't take to stumbling over each other and competing for the shower and desk for a sustained period of time. The hotel-type food service is both too expensive and too limited for the long term seminar. And tying up blocks of rooms for weeks or months makes it difficult to schedule in the shorter conferences economically and efficiently. We're beginning to think about remodeling, adding a long-term seminar wing, or designing a whole new facility to accommodate the trend toward sustained seminars that won't replace but will add to our shorter conferences and institutes."

## NEED PRESIDENTIAL SUPPORT

"I think we ought to realize that there is a great deal to be done and we don't necessarily know how to do it," said Arthur Adams of the University of New Hampshire. "You talk about new facilities to meet new trends. We're still trying to finance the initial building of the New England Center. As a former university president, I'm very aware that the central administration has not been very concerned about Continuing Education. The problem is that the budgets of the universities are built almost exclusively around on-campus instruction. I think it's rather clear that in the places where Continuing Education has prospered, the president of the university has been personally involved, as, for instance, President Hannah at Michigan State, President Aderhold at Georgia, President Hardin at Nebraska and President Cross at Oklahoma.

"But, as Paul Miller, assistant secretary for education in the Department of Health, Education and Welfare, said at a New England Center Conference on Extension Activities, 'There is a collision of forces taking place in the life of the American university today, involving on the one hand the 1000 years of tradition and sentiment about a university, that it could serve best if it remained disengaged from society, and on the other hand the contemporary concerns of an urban industrial society which thrives on knowledge and is calling upon the university not to disengage but rather to seek an engagement with the public process.' Miller saw two worlds in the university: the faculty holding tenaciously to the traditional historic sentiment; the administrators accommodating to the contemporary needs of society in order to get support for the university. And Miller's conclusion was simply that Continuing Education was going to have to be budgeted as a normal function of an institution much like research and teaching and that, in order to exist, universities were going to have to find straightforward ways of helping Continuing Education to stand on its own feet."

"There's a third force at work in Continuing Education," said Frank Jessup, Secretary of the Delegacy for Extra-Mural Studies at the University

Frank Jessup

of Oxford. "Universities do accumulate knowledge and ideas and wisdom, and they have a duty to share them with the rest of society. But you know there is a mutuality in the sharing, and knowledge and ideas and wisdom do not flow only in one direction. Society is infringing on the campus just as the campus is moving into the market place. I think it needs to be said of us in Continuing Education as it was said of Chaucer's parson, 'Gladly would he learn, and gladly teach.' At Oxford we look forward to our residential adult education Centre becoming a Centre for reciprocity in learning."

## NEW VIEW OF "COLLEGE DROP-OUT"

"Actually," said Oklahoma Assistant Dean, Jess Burkett, "we're going to have to redefine the term 'college drop-out.' We used to think a drop-out was one who didn't complete his study for a baccalaureate degree and that the man who did get the degree, or later went on to get a graduate degree, had finished his education.

"In the future it seems to me that the college graduate who doesn't return periodically for Continuing Education will also have to be classified as 'college drop-out.' I think that there are three interrelated strands of Continuing Education: remedial or second chance programs; those programs designed to meet the developmental tests of adulthood; and the Continuing

Education of college graduates to keep abreast of new knowledge in their fields of scholarship or professional competence."

## THE SUMMING-UP

"Perhaps what we're thinking can be summed-up," said Professor Houle, "by saying that a sound program of education is not a piece of carpentry to be put together in a few days; it is like a tree which must be allowed to grow and mature—a simple but powerful idea of lifelong learning for all men. I think we feel that the team concept of the Continuing Education Center, in which staff, faculty, facility and community work together to conceive appropriate and effective programs, is an important contribution to the search for ways to achieve this ideal. I think we're agreed that the residential experience combined with other methods of study and learning is an important aspect of Continuing Education. I think we're agreed that the Studies and Training Programs in adult education, which have been undertaken by a number of our universities, are essential and fruitful methods for developing knowledgeable and dedicated practitioners for Continuing Education and for engendering rigorous research into the needs and processes of adult learning as well as evaluating the practices and procedures through which we seek to assist the learning process. Finally, I think we all feel that while a central task of Continuing Education is vocational and professional in-service education throughout life, we still feel that life is so rich that learning should not be restricted to a single compartment. Adulthood stretches out before us; it is the time when our powers of learning are at their peak, when we are freed of the necessities of formal schooling and when we may pursue to our own benefit and to the benefit of society the special kinds of learning which give to life its interest and its savor. This, then, is where we began, where we are, and where we are going."